INTERCULTURAL COMMUNICATION FOR THE GLOBAL BUSINESS PROFESSIONAL

This text integrates business and communication concepts to immerse students in the global communication experiences of business professionals.

The authors argue that the essentials of intercultural communication, such as nonverbal communication, conflict, meeting management, interviewing, and negotiations, are most useful to burgeoning professionals when they are woven into discussions about economic systems, market forces, production processes, finance structures, and human resources priorities. Each chapter begins with an explanation of theories and key terms appropriate for introductory-level students in both business and communication, then supplements that discussion with examples that demonstrate the concepts at work. The cases chosen represent different market systems in both dominant and emerging economies, explaining the cultures of competitive markets with a global perspective rather than focusing on the United States.

This book is ideal as a text for courses in international business or professional intercultural communication, or as a supplement for more general business and communication courses.

Mara K. Berkland is Professor of Communication at North Central College, Naperville, Illinois.

Amy Grim Buxbaum is Associate Professor of Communication at North Central College, Naperville, Illinois.

INTERCULTURAL COMMUNICATION FOR THE GLOBAL BUSINESS PROFESSIONAL

Edited by
Mara K. Berkland and Amy Grim Buxbaum

NEW YORK AND LONDON

Designed cover image: Christoph Burgstedt / © Getty Images

First published 2024
by Routledge
605 Third Avenue, New York, NY 10158

and by Routledge
4 Park Square, Milton Park, Abingdon, Oxon, OX14 4RN

Routledge is an imprint of the Taylor & Francis Group, an informa business

© 2024 selection and editorial matter, Mara K. Berkland and Amy Grim Buxbaum; individual chapters, the contributors

The right of Mara K. Berkland and Amy Grim Buxbaum to be identified as the authors of the editorial material, and of the authors for their individual chapters, has been asserted in accordance with sections 77 and 78 of the Copyright, Designs and Patents Act 1988.

All rights reserved. No part of this book may be reprinted or reproduced or utilised in any form or by any electronic, mechanical, or other means, now known or hereafter invented, including photocopying and recording, or in any information storage or retrieval system, without permission in writing from the publishers.

Trademark notice: Product or corporate names may be trademarks or registered trademarks, and are used only for identification and explanation without intent to infringe.

Library of Congress Cataloging-in-Publication Data
Names: Berkland, Mara Kathleen, editor. | Buxbaum, Amy Grim, editor.
Title: Intercultural communication for the global business professional / edited by Mara K. Berkland and Amy Grim Buxbaum.
Description: New York, NY : Routledge, 2024. | Includes bibliographical references and index.
Identifiers: LCCN 2023023116 (print) | LCCN 2023023117 (ebook) | ISBN 9781032285399 (paperback) | ISBN 9781032287157 (hardback) | ISBN 9781003298199 (ebook)
Subjects: LCSH: Communication in management—Cross-cultural studies. | km Business communication—Cross-cultural studies. | Intercultural communication.
Classification: LCC HD30.3 .I554 2024 (print) | LCC HD30.3 (ebook) | DDC 658.4/5—dc23/eng/20230629
LC record available at https://lccn.loc.gov/2023023116
LC ebook record available at https://lccn.loc.gov/2023023117

ISBN: 9781032287157 (hbk)
ISBN: 9781032285399 (pbk)
ISBN: 9781003298199 (ebk)

DOI: 10.4324/9781003298199

Typeset in Galliard
by codeMantra

To Richard Paine,
for putting us on the same place on the planet

CONTENTS

List of Figures ix
List of Tables xi
List of Contributors xiii
Overview of the Chapters xvii
Acknowledgments xxiii

Introduction 1

1 Fostering Intercultural Understanding for the Global
  Business Professional 3
  Mara K. Berkland, Amy Grim Buxbaum and Supna Jain

PART I
Interpersonal Contexts 19

2 Cultural Differences in the Display of Emotion
  During the Hiring Process 21
  Chi Cheng Lao and Lucy Zhang Bencharit

3 Cultural Norms of Turn-Taking in English and
  Chinese Conversations 34
  Weihua Zhu

4 Cultural Variations in Politeness Strategies Used
  in Email Communication 45
  Chanki Moon

PART II
Group and Organizational Contexts   59

5 Perceptions of Coworker Trustworthiness in Japan and the United States   61
Masami Nishishiba

6 Cultural Dimensions of Organizational Loyalty in Germany and China   74
Stephan Meschke and Juana Du

7 Leveraging Culture to Confront Sexual Harassment in a Multicultural Organization   87
Amy Grim Buxbaum and Mara K. Berkland

PART III
Institutional Contexts   103

8 Cultural Tourism and Retail Store Aesthetics in Norway and Morocco   105
Mara K. Berkland

9 Cultural Comparison of Currency Demand in Argentina and India   117
Brenden J. Mason and Kabir Dasgupta

10 Cultural Interpretation of International Financial Reporting Standards in the Anglo-Saxon and Continental Models of Accounting   130
Katarzyna Koleśnik and Sylwia Silska-Gembka

Conclusion   145

11 Cultural Influence and Ethical Considerations for the Global Business Professional   147
Mara K. Berkland and Amy Grim Buxbaum

Index   *159*

FIGURES

1.1	The four key elements of culture	5
2.1	Differences in smile intensity between European American (left) and HK Chinese (right)	27
2.2	Facial expressions showing excited, calm, and neutral states	30
3.1	A model of context, practice, and perception (Zhu, 2019, p. 14)	42
8.1	A shop in Fez Medina, Morocco	109
8.2	Details of Juhl's Silver Gallery, Kautokeino, Norway	110
9.1	Currency as a fraction of GDP and interest rate on savings deposits	121
9.2	Close substitutes for currency: Argentina (ARG) and India (IND)	123
10.1	Conservatism vs. optimism and probability threshold for items increasing financial results (Gierusz et al., 2022)	139
10.2	Conservatism vs. optimism and probability threshold for items decreasing financial results (Gierusz et al., 2022)	139
10.3	Secrecy vs. transparency and probability threshold for making disclosures in the financial statement (Gierusz et al., 2022)	141

TABLES

2.1	Examples of word stems indicating excited or calm states	26
2.2	Examples of written responses indicating excited and calm emotions	26
5.1	Terms linked to trustworthiness	64
5.2	Trustworthiness groupings by Japanese businesspeople	66
5.3	Trustworthiness groupings by US businesspeople	67
6.1	Employee loyalty concept (Exploratory Factor Analysis, German sample)	77
6.2	Employee loyalty concept with negative outcomes (correlations, German sample)	78
6.3	Initial approach of employee loyalty concept for East Asian cultures (Exploratory Factor Analysis, Chinese sample)	79
6.4	Employee loyalty concept with negative outcomes (correlations, Chinese sample)	79
10.1	Gray's theoretical framework of cultural aspects of accounting	132
10.2	Relationships between Gray's accounting values and Hofstede's cultural dimensions	133
10.3	Conversion of Hofstede data to Gray's conservatism and secrecy accounting values for Poland and the UK	136

CONTRIBUTORS

Lucy Zhang Bencharit (PhD, Stanford University) is an Assistant Professor in the Department of Psychology and Child Development at California Polytechnic State University, San Luis Obispo, California. Her research aims to promote positive outcomes for diverse groups in employment, workplace, and classroom settings. She is broadly interested in how cultural factors may subtly and unconsciously shape our behaviors, judgments, and decision-making.

Mara K. Berkland (PhD, University of Utah) is a Professor of Communication at North Central College in Naperville, Illinois. Trained in sociolinguistics, her research focuses on effective communication and the socialization of people through language and cultures, both national and disciplinary. Her recent publications address the issues of disciplinary socialization as cross-cultural research, linguistic adaptation within women's rights reform, and immediacy strategies within education.

Amy Grim Buxbaum (PhD, University of Colorado) is an Associate Professor of Communication at North Central College in Naperville, Illinois. Her work lies at the intersection of rhetoric and organizational communication, specifically how organizational cultural practices invite or inhibit democratic discourse and the way media frames workplace issues. Most recently, she has contributed to Project Censored's *State of the Free Press* annuals.

Kabir Dasgupta (PhD, Temple University) is a Senior Economist at the Federal Reserve Board of Governors, Washington DC. His primary research interests lie in applied welfare economics and the human capital outcomes of public policy.

Juana Du (PhD, Hong Kong Baptist University) is an Associate Professor in the School of Communication and Culture at Royal Roads University, Victoria, BC, Canada. Her research interests include improving intercultural communication in a globalized world, cross-cultural adaptation of international students, expatriate training and relocation, organizational communication, diversity and culture, organizational learning, and knowledge management.

Supna Jain (JD, DePaul University) is Senior Lecturer of Communication at North Central College in Naperville, Illinois. She applies her professional and educational experience in interpersonal and visual communication to persuasion and social change cultural contexts. Her recent publications address the issues of gender inequity and the cultural strategies used to challenge them.

Katarzyna Koleśnik (PhD, University of Gdańsk) is faculty in the Department of Accounting at the University of Gdańsk, Gdańsk, Poland. Her main research interests are interdisciplinary, grounded in the areas of international accounting and sustainability reporting, with a specific emphasis on cultural and religious aspects of financial and nonfinancial disclosures.

Chi Cheng Lao is currently a doctoral student in the Clinical Psychology program at Palo Alto University in California and a crisis line specialist at Central Coast Hotline in California. She graduated from California Polytechnic State University with a BS. in Psychology with minors in Child Development, Statistics, and Women's and Gender Studies.

Brenden J. Mason (PhD, Temple University) is an Assistant Professor of Economics at North Central College in Naperville, Illinois. His primary research interests lie in applied welfare economics and the human capital outcomes of public policy. His most recent research focuses on the impacts of the shadow economy on electronic currency and the role that interest rates play in bankruptcy.

Stephan Meschke (PhD, Technische Universität Bergakademie Freiberg) is a postdoctoral researcher at Technische Universität Bergakademie Freiberg in Germany. His multidisciplinary work at the interface of academia and industry ranges from intercultural employee loyalty to research cooperation and commercialization of academic innovations. His experience includes head of a research transfer department, founder of scientific spin-off companies, and a trainer for industry and academia.

Chanki Moon (PhD, University of Kent) is an Assistant Professor of Social Psychology and Criminology at Royal Holloway, University of London, London, and co-directs its Institute for the Study of Power, Crime, and Society. Moon's research focuses on how individuals' values and norms as well as emotional, cognitive, and behavioral outcomes associated with power and status in interpersonal/intergroup relationships can be shaped by cultural settings.

Masami Nishishiba (PhD, Portland State University) is Department Chair and Professor in the Department of Public Administration at the Mark O. Hatfield School of Government, Portland State University in Portland, Oregon, where she also serves as Associate Director of the Center for Public Service at the Hatfield School of Government. Her research interests include issues of social diversity, civic capacity, government–citizen interface, and comparative local government.

Sylwia Silska-Gembka (PhD, University of Gdańsk) is faculty in the Department of Accounting at the University of Gdańsk, Gdańsk, Poland. Her research focuses on ethical and cultural determinants of accounting. Her recent publications address the issues of accounting ethics and the influence of culture on accounting judgment.

Weihua Zhu (PhD, University of Florida) is Associate Professor of Chinese Linguistics at the University of Wisconsin–Madison, Madison, Wisconsin. Her current research interests include interactional features of Mandarin Chinese speakers in natural conversation, speech behavior and pragmatic perception, and teaching Chinese as a foreign language. She has recently published a series of articles on the differences in turn-taking and topic-changing between English and Chinese speakers.

OVERVIEW OF THE CHAPTERS

Introduction

Chapter 1
Fostering Intercultural Understanding for the Global Business Professional
Mara K. Berkland, Amy Grim Buxbaum, and Supna Jain

Intercultural communication, within or across organizations, is multilayered and complex. Despite the cultural complexity that is present in any intercultural interaction, organizations and professionals are able to work and reach positive outcomes by working across cultural boundaries, more specifically by becoming more familiar with cultural differences and how they impact interactions, processes, and decision-making. This chapter presents an overview of the theory of cultural systems by explaining its properties and functions within the context of national cultures and how national cultural systems impact the ideological framework, codified by interactions, and symbol systems in which global professionals interact. It then previews the international and interdisciplinary contributions of this volume. The goal is to expose young business professionals to a variety of crosscultural interactions and to show how cultures may view the same business norm differently. Understanding the nuances of cross-cultural interactions will foster more effective professional communication in global business contexts.

Part 1: Interpersonal Contexts

Chapter 2
Cultural Differences in the Display of Emotion during the Hiring Process
Chi Cheng Lao and Lucy Zhang Bencharit

Hiring decisions are often assumed to be based on merit; however, as hiring mangers interpret emotional cues during the hiring process, they may be unintentionally limiting the diversity of their workforce. Because employers may not be aware of the way their culture's ideal emotions influence their judgments, they may view an applicant with different emotional values as unqualified rather than valuing emotional expressions that are different from their own. Specifically, preferences for excitement over calm or vice versa are based on cultural background. In a European American environment, an applicant can increase their chances with a European American employer or company if they express more excitement. However, excited emotional expression in a Hong Kong Chinese environment may put the candidate at risk of being passed over.

Chapter 3
Cultural Norms of Turn-Taking in English and Chinese Conversations
Weihua Zhu

Turn-taking in conversation is a speaker's stretch of speech to which other people listen. Whether long or short, at the end of the turn, the next speaker begins a turn. Understanding appropriate turn-taking so as to not interrupt or offend is an important skill in business interactions. Professionals who speak American English and Mandarin Chinese share some commonalities, however differ in the degree to which they will overlap or interrupt a speaker. Because of this difference, speakers from these two different cultures, when working together, might encounter communication breakdowns or misunderstandings, which can potentially damage their professional relationship. This chapter explores the ways that such miscommunication might lead to adverse consequences when professionals are not aware of cross-cultural differences in the organization of conversational turn-taking.

Chapter 4
Cultural Variations in Politeness Strategies Used in Email Communication
Chanki Moon

Being polite is important for creating and sustaining successful professional relationships. Because politeness norms vary across cultures, cultural differences in the communication of politeness may create misunderstanding. Individuals in East Asian cultures tend to use more high-context communication styles that are based on relational concerns and politeness principles, while people in Western cultures tend to use more low-context communication styles that entail being more open and precise. This study of email communication shows how cultural differences exist in the linguistic expression of politeness regarding face concerns. While members of East Asian societies tend to use more apology expressions, members of Western societies tend to use more gratitude expressions. Since communication styles and politeness strategies vary from culture to culture, it is important for business professionals to enhance their understanding of these cultural norms as they communicate with others in a globalized world.

Part 2: Group and Organizational Contexts

Chapter 5
Perceptions of Co-Worker Trustworthiness in Japan and the United States
Masami Nishishiba

The creation and maintenance of trust in professional relationships is key to successful business relationships. Interactants look for cues that reflect trustworthiness; however, those cues vary based on cultural values and worldview orientations. The research described in this chapter identifies important differences between Japanese and U.S. concepts of trustworthiness in business. Japanese business professionals tended to give greater emphasis to organizational commitment as a sign of trustworthiness, while U.S. business professionals tended to give greater emphasis to personal integrity as an autonomous individual. These differences correspond to cultural orientations on a collectivism/individualism scale and interdependent/independent views of trustworthiness. Better understanding of such variance among intercultural partners may help improve professional communication as well as organizational well-being.

Chapter 6
Cultural Dimensions of Organizational Loyalty in Germany and China
Stephan Meschke and Juana Du

This chapter offers fresh insights on employee loyalty, from an intercultural perspective of the differences between Chinese and German employees who respond to expectations of overwork or overtime differently. The behavior of work overload resulting from high employee loyalty is markedly different in the two cultures and should also be managed differently. While work overload is interpreted as negative employee behavior in German companies, it is regarded as very positive behavior in Chinese companies. This underscores why loyalty constructs cannot have universal validity but must be adapted to the different cultural characteristics in each case. From the perspective of business managers, companies need to develop strategies and organizational procedures to support employee loyalty as a way to better leverage employee loyalty as competitive advantage. From the perspective of employees, we suggest they develop cross-cultural understanding of employee loyalty and its relationship with workplace performance. It is a good starting point to cultivate intercultural competence to work in multicultural teams and organizations.

Chapter 7
Leveraging Culture to Confront Sexual Harassment in a Multicultural Organization
Amy Grim Buxbaum and Mara K. Berkland

This chapter examines a unique workplace in the Netherlands where employees from diverse national cultural backgrounds respond to an alleged incident of sexual harassment in their organization. The case shows how members of a multinational team leveraged their knowledge of their organization's national host culture in order to create a message that is critical of management and simultaneously establishes its own legitimacy to speak on the complex and difficult issue of sexual harassment. Their formal response to organizational statements illustrates the ways multinational employee teams can harness the cultural values of their company to advocate for change.

Part 3: Institutional Contexts

Chapter 8
Cultural Tourism and Retail Store Aesthetics in Norway and Morocco
Mara K. Berkland

Tolerance for uncertainty is just one of the dimensions that can explain how shoppers go about selecting goods or how retailers set up the buying experience for cultural tourists. Reducing uncertainty means reducing risk, whether the risk be financial (spending more than the value), functional (does not meet the need or work as assumed or promised), physical (personal illness or injury as a consequence of misunderstanding cultural cues), social (inauthentic or of poor quality that may be noticed by others), or psychological (damages self-esteem by making the traveler seem gullible or vulnerable). Of Hofstede's five cultural dimensions, uncertainty avoidance is considered the most influential ideological frame related to travel shopping because tourists are already disequilibrated by being outside of their home cultures. Comparing Moroccan store layouts with those found in Norway illustrates the differences between tolerances for uncertainty.

Chapter 9
Cultural Comparison of Currency Demand in Argentina and India
Brenden J. Mason and Kabir Dasgupta

Income, prices, interest rates, and uncertainty play major roles in the demand for currency. Technology and credit also affect the demand for cash. As income increases, the demand for cash increases, especially income that is earned in the shadow economy. This chapter explores two countries with large shadow economies: Argentina and India. Argentina's economic history is filled with bouts of high inflation, including in recent times. India's shadow economy is possibly the largest on earth, the foundation of which is cash. Recently, these two countries experienced an infrequent economic phenomenon—the introduction of new banknotes—creating a unique opportunity to study them in comparison and the population's response to the monetary change. Despite the peso's rapidly falling value, the Argentine government issued new bills so that consumers could fund their purchases. India demonetized, taking high-denomination notes out of circulation and substituting them for new ones, all in an attempt to thwart the tax-evading effects of the shadow economy.

Chapter 10
Cultural Interpretation of International Financial Reporting Standards in the Anglo-Saxon and Continental Models of Accounting
Katarzyna Koleśnik and Sylwia Silska-Gembka

Despite the expectation that accounting is objective, a number of decisions need to be made when reporting profit and loss and disclosing transactions. National culture must be considered when examining the judgments made by accountants when making such decisions. Polish and British cultures have historically different ideological perspectives which are considered when interpreting selected International Financial Reporting Standards (IFRS) in the Anglo-Saxon and continental models of accounting. As researchers have studied the question of accounting conservatism and secrecy across cultures, they have found some evidence of increasing similarity in accounting judgments, perhaps because of global interaction and the creation of IFRS. Studies addressing non-European countries persist in showing greater differences, but the continued interdependency of European Union (EU) member countries, including citizen mobility, shared political discussions, and the ease of developing transnational corporations in the EU, has demonstrated that culture is more fluid and diverse than national borders might imply. This chapter shows that continental EU members may be less conservative after IFRS adoption.

Conclusion

Chapter 11
Cultural Influence and Ethical Considerations for the Global Business Professional
Mara K. Berkland and Amy Grim Buxbaum

After summarizing the contributions of each chapter, this concluding chapter explains the process of cultural influence and considers the ethical issues it raises when professionals engage in cross-cultural interactions. Beyond business effectiveness, there is much more to consider when entering into an intercultural interaction, especially when one considers differences in power and needs characteristic of organizations engaged in global commerce. When an organization is situated within the boundaries of a national culture that may not have the resources or infrastructure to fully support its people, then cultural ideology, values, norms, and codes may be sacrificed in order to adapt to the organization that presents necessary and valuable resources. Such adaptations potentially contribute to the loss of cultural diversity around the globe, not only in terms of languages but in terms of values and ideologies. As global professionals engage in multicultural interactions, they should be mindful not only of cultural variance but of the potential consequences for their own and other cultures.

ACKNOWLEDGMENTS

We wish to acknowledge North Central College and its commitment to creating an environment where teachers can also be scholars. In addition to appreciating the institutional support, we especially want to honor the cadre of women colleagues and leaders at our college who wore the path before and alongside us. You may not have known it, but your mere presence, perseverance, and strength inspire us.

Thank you to our contributors for giving us the opportunity to explore interdisciplinary scholarship and voices from around the globe. We hope this text reveals the breadth of important perspectives that warrant our attention as we engage with others in a multicultural professional world. Additionally, without our editor, Felisa Salvago-Keyes, this book would certainly not exist. What started as a conversation about a text needed for a course ended in this volume. Her patience, encouragement, and direction gave us confidence.

Finally, we are grateful for our dear colleagues, friends, and families, whose support allowed us the time, space, and faith to complete this project.

Introduction

1
FOSTERING INTERCULTURAL UNDERSTANDING FOR THE GLOBAL BUSINESS PROFESSIONAL

Mara K. Berkland, Amy Grim Buxbaum and Supna Jain

Business professionals often understand that partners from different cultures will perceive interactions differently or may communicate in different ways, but the human mind cannot fully imagine scenarios outside of our own experiences. When we encounter others whose cultural orientations foster norms for behaviors that are different from our own, we often struggle to understand, much less empathize. Although businesses have become increasingly aware of the need for cultural competence, often professional training about cultural sensitivity focuses on simple symbols of cultural difference such as handshakes, clothing, or expressions. Those superficial manifestations of culture are important, but only insofar as they are explored as representative symbols of larger cultural perspectives that color a host of professional interactions. How employees are hired, contracts are negotiated, meetings are run, and currency is traded, for example, are grounded in the priorities and values of a cultural system. When business relationships, projects, or negotiations are at the forefront of the interaction, the potential consequences of misunderstanding are great.

This text strives to expose early career business professionals to a variety of cross-cultural interactions and to show how cultures may view the same business norm differently. We want students to understand the specific examples and theoretical explanations in each chapter so that they are better able to appreciate the nuances of cross-cultural interactions, which we hope will foster more effective professional communication in global business contexts.

DOI: 10.4324/9781003298199-2

What Is Culture?

In general, culture is an ideological framework that becomes codified by interactions, creating a symbolic system that makes interactions comprehensible and somewhat predictable (Geertz, 1973). When cultures intersect in professional settings, cross-cultural communication becomes even more multilayered and complex. Yet, despite the complexity and the layers of differences that might be present in any intercultural interaction, organizations and professionals can learn to work across cultural boundaries and reach positive business outcomes. By becoming more cognizant of cultural differences and how they impact interactions, processes, and decision-making, professionals are better able to maintain international professional relationships (Hofstede, 1980; Lindorff, 2010).

One way that communicators can become familiar with cultural differences is by determining the cultural components that are potentially in tension. Making sense of the complex components of culture as they are revealed in real-world interactions, however, is a daunting task. Identifying the theoretically consistent dimensions of cultures within diverse organizations of relatively homogenous societies is also challenging. Bringing those two analyses together and learning to identify cultural markers as they manifest within organizations from different nations and societies—cross-cultural organizational interaction—is the challenge pursued in this text.

The first step in the process of figuring out where potential misunderstanding may lie is to identify how cultures guide the thinking of the people in the interaction. Put simply: Cultural systems foster coherence and comprehension. People who interact regularly share common symbols and sets of behaviors so that they can effectively carry out the business of survival. Cultures maintain coherence by rewarding behaviors and ideas that align with the larger, predominantly unspoken, ideological framework. Reinforcing coherent ideals and symbols gives the participants tools for common understanding. In other words, if everyone understands that a particular idea is important or that a certain symbol means a specific thing, cultural members can rely on that tacitly shared knowledge to transmit ideas accurately and efficiently. This system is taught formally and informally to cultural newcomers.

Cultural Systems

Four key elements comprise every cultural system: codes, norms, values, and ideology. Like an ecosystem, the four elements work together to reflect and reaffirm each other in their repetition across interactions. Codes reflect and reinforce norms, values, and ideology, just as ideology will trickle into values, norms, and codes. The repetition of codes, norms, and values, when

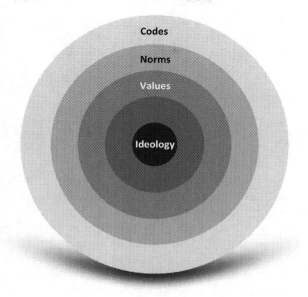

FIGURE 1.1 The four key elements of culture

frequent and far reaching, will strengthen ideological position, cultural values, and commitment to "correct" behavior (Hall, Covarrubias, & Kirschbaum, 2017). Similar to the layers found in a body of water, the four layers or components interact symbiotically, reinforcing and building upon each other, nourishing and permeating each component through interdependence.

Code

Every culture has a unique sign system, or *code*, which is the most concrete element in the cultural ecosystem. A code is the combining of signs to create complex informational exchanges. Signs are resources that help us to interact with each other by providing shorthand for an idea or concept. Each sign holds a multifaceted meaning that contains not only dictionary-level meaning but also socio-emotional cues. Codes are frequently embedded with cultural ideology; meaning comes not just from the individual sign but from the set of signs within which it appears.

For example, the color green is a sign that can mean "go", or "eco-friendly", or "envy", or "new", or "money", depending on its symbolic context. The specific meaning of "green" becomes clear only in relation to other signs in a code, such as those found at an intersection, in the grocery store, or in a social group or business setting. When strung together, signs create a code that allows those who use it to exchange complicated and meaningful ideas. Examples of such sign systems, or codes, include language, gestures, food, clothing, sounds, or design. In real life, just as no one sign stands alone, codes must be understood in terms of their combinations in specific contexts.

Norms

Norms are the social rules for behavior, in terms of both what is allowed and what is not. Although some norms are explicitly stated as rules (e.g., raise your hand to be called upon before speaking), most norms reflect taken-for-granted assumptions that guide behavior (e.g., the person of higher social status speaks first—or last—in a meeting). Norms guide how people are expected to behave in a given context, what they are expected to say, the order events are expected to happen, and the appropriate symbols to display at certain times. Generally, these unspoken social rules are understood by members of a group, and it is the shared group understanding that perpetuates their routine use and persistence. Norms often integrate codes, and so too does their formal enactment reflect social values and ideologies.

Values

Values are explicit manifestations of the ideals of a culture. They are the model aspirations that humans often voice using the word "should". Values are often publicly pronounced, and cultural members regard them as the guiding force for their behavior and decision-making (i.e., individuality, equality). Values are also deeply rooted and illustrate what a system holds as most important, even if the average member of the culture, or the system itself, cannot (yet) perform to the standard. Symbols and norms often reflect values, but sometimes norms and symbols can fail to meet the highest ideals clarified by the system's values. As a result of this lack of correspondence, conflict can emerge within the system.

Ideology

In general, *ideology* refers to the dominantly held mindset of a given group of people. Shared mindsets can be found in any group ranging from small ones such as families and social circles to larger entities like audiences, organizations, or entire nations. Ideology provides the basic assumptions that guide the structure and priorities of a system (i.e., capitalism). Not everything can be equally important in a culture, and ideology clarifies what the order of importance should be. This element of culture is the most abstract and is often invisible to the group members until ideological commitments are made visible through the introduction of a contrast or comparison. The ideology of a culture permeates its values, norms, and codes, just as the values, norms, and codes reinforce one another through repetition.

Cultural Socialization

Cultural systems run smoothly because their participants are constantly socialized. Socialization into a culture happens immediately upon entrance into the system (i.e., birth or immigration for national cultures, orientation for organizational cultures). As cultural newcomers are exposed to the codes and norms of the system, they are corrected and directed regarding the rules of correct performance. As participants encounter new subsystems (i.e., schools, families, government agencies), or organizations encounter national cultures (i.e., branches, divisions, teams, or corporate ranks in organizational cultures), they will develop a more nuanced and deeper understanding of the layers that exist in a cultural system.

It helps to think of socialization as a series of exposures over time. There are myriad ideas, concepts, or perspectives in the world, but socialization is the process of being exposed to the specific ones that are prioritized or recognized by the dominant cultural group. Cultural newcomers and insiders alike are rewarded for understanding and performing them correctly. Increased exposure to an idea or perspective leads to feelings of familiarity, normalcy, and acceptance. As a result, newcomers begin to think less about it as being "a perspective", and more as "the way things are", or even as the "truth".

Unique Cultural Systems

National cultures and organizational cultures are both cultural systems that can exist simultaneously and interact in interesting ways. When they intersect in business settings, there are a variety of ways they can be expressed in professional interactions, which can potentially create confusion. In organizations, for example, members of a shared organizational culture might encounter other members who come from diverse national cultures. Within national cultures, members of different organizational or professional cultures might be called to work with each other. And, in the most complex cases, members of organizations from one national culture might be invited to work with members of a different organization from a different national culture. At work in these interactions are two very dominant systems of socialization, each with its ideologies, values, norms, and codes: the national culture and the professional culture. While, theoretically, cultural systems have the same four foundations—ideology, values, norms, and codes—they can look quite different in action.

National Cultures and Worldview Orientations

National cultures are defined by geopolitical boundaries. Recognizing the shared history, values, norms, and identity of a nation-state is a helpful first step in understanding culture. In addition to national culture, geographic areas consist of co-cultures that may have even greater similarities to one another because of their proximity and shared social experiences. There are a number of political and social structures (e.g., schools, governments, transit systems, economic systems) that pull culture to the edge of these boundaries and provide structure to broader co-cultural systems and maintain consistency across a people. Geographic boundaries are not necessarily barriers to cultural practices, languages, or beliefs, which can and do spread across formal national lines.

Ideological frameworks of nations have been historically explained by cultural scholars through the lens of worldview orientations. Worldviews espouse a set of tacit truths humans hold about which ways of being should be prioritized. These truths sit along a continuum, and members of a culture generally occupy the same position on the continuum as others in their culture, although certainly there is individual variation. Within a cultural system, worldviews are rarely explicitly acknowledged or interrogated, as they operate at an unconscious taken-for-granted level that shapes human understanding of the world. According to Hall, Covarrubias, and Kirschbaum (2017), worldviews are best thought of as "answers to basic human questions" about the way the social world behaves, and cultural members navigate prioritization along the spectrum by increasing or decreasing the level of degree toward a priority.

Scholars have proposed a number of worldview continua (Hall, 1959; Hofstede, 1991; House et al., 2004). Currently, multiple interpretations of cultural value dimensions exist, and Hofstede's (1991) dimensions are the most well-known. Hall's (1959) cultural dimensions highlight a unique understanding of different communication styles, and the recent Global Leadership and Organizational Behavior Effectiveness (GLOBE) dimensions focus specifically on cultural dimensions and their connections to leadership (House et al., 2004). Combined, these scholarly approaches provide insight into the nature of cultural and professional decision-making. This volume focuses on the dimensions that commonly create misunderstandings in cross-cultural interactions:

- individualism/collectivism
- hierarchy/egalitarianism
- monochronic/polychronic

- high context/low context
- ascription/achievement
- mastery/adaptive

Individualism/Collectivism Dimension

The individualism/collectivism dimension is one of the most studied worldview orientations and is credited for creating the most confusion in intercultural communication within both professional and personal contexts. This continuum highlights the negotiation of group and individual importance, and it underlies decisions about the allocation of resources such as material goods, identities, esteem, or loyalty.

A strong collectivist orientation prioritizes the well-being and identity of the group, whereas the individualist orientation puts more value on the development and autonomy of the individual. Collectivism and individualism are important concepts in cultures because they highlight the tension between the need to get along and work together with the desire to cultivate oneself and be unique. Collectivism favors group harmony and solidarity, while individualism favors self-interest. For example, a culture that has a strong orientation toward individualism will likely espouse values such as "people should speak their minds" or "people should be self-sufficient", whereas collectivist cultures will hold values such as "people should be loyal" and defer to community or organizational norms.

Some norms that might reflect a national cultural orientation would be the use of public transit which prioritizes a system that serves most of the population versus, for example, the individual comforts and time control (and resource use) of an automobile, or whether we give awards or compensation predominantly to individuals or disperse accolades to the entire team. Codes might emphasize an individual's occupation or first name versus a family group or organization. Additionally, words like "independence" and "dependence" may have different connotative meanings based on the worldview orientation of the national culture in which they are used.

Hierarchy/Egalitarian Dimension

Another worldview dimension that frequently creates conflict is the one that addresses human value. The hierarchy/egalitarian dimension assesses the worth of people in a society. The strongest leaning hierarchical societies hold that the inherent value of people is not equal and that some people are more or less important to the cultural system by virtue of their position in the social hierarchy. The strongest leaning egalitarian societies believe that all humans have equal worth, regardless of their position in the social hierarchy.

By looking at the cultural norms surrounding resource distribution (i.e., wage equity, provision of education, equal application of rule of law), it is possible to see the norms that reflect a culture's commitment to human value. The ideological framework is often codified with use of titles, rather than names, and organizational or legal paperwork might even spell out different ways of categorizing people and the rewards they get for those different ranks.

One clear area of tension related to hierarchy and egalitarianism in professional contexts is the perception of workplace bullying. Bullying at work has largely been evaluated from a European or American lens and has defined acts of bullying as hostile verbal or nonverbal behaviors such as harassing, insulting, or ostracizing someone or their work. However, Lian et al. (2012) found that employees with higher comfort with hierarchy or power distance orientation were less likely to view abusive supervision as problematic, unfair, or threatening to relationships. Essentially, globalization has presented the possibility for misunderstanding in ways that were not necessarily anticipated when it comes to the perception of bullying. As employees and managers from different cultures interact more frequently, through a variety of channels, research has found that people from different cultures perceive management styles, strategies, or requests differently. What to one culture may be a direct criticism or a frequent request to work more hours from a manager may seem like bullying behavior to another (Salin et al., 2019).

Ascription/Achievement Dimension

The ascription/achievement dimension highlights the relative importance of either birthright or effort to a person's social position. Often characterized as the dimension of social mobility, this dimension clarifies the tension that exists in systems where hard work or personal merit predicts one's social place or whether that place is relatively fixed based on inherited status. Whether people are encouraged to change beyond their group of origin, especially in terms of social or economic status, is often a value tied to this dimension. Normatively, mingling of people from different stations or statuses might be encouraged or discouraged, and the encoding of these differences might be specific names of people (castes, religions, professions) or even locales (regions, neighborhoods, clubs) that express a fixed identity.

High-Context/Low-Context Dimension

The high-context/low-context dimension speaks to the importance of shared knowledge among members of a culture. Edward Hall (1959), who coined the terms "high context" and "low context", explains this spectrum as the location of information. High-context communication expects that the information necessary to understand a situation or exchange is already inside that person. In contrast, low-context communication presumes that information must be explicitly provided via the appropriate codes. In many ways, this dimension is relationship dependent. In low-context communication, the connection between communication partners or setting does not matter; communication is expected to be direct, clear, and full of information. High-context communication assumes a significant level of shared knowledge. It relies on minimal verbal clarification because communication partners are presumed to already share background information. Normatively, cultures might link the sharing of information verbally to either trustworthiness or untrustworthiness, and the amount of information included in explicitly written code (e.g., instructions, contracts, invitations) will reaffirm the commitment to the ideology.

For example, recent research on global virtual teams (GVTs) found that differences in context orientation require different communication strategies so as not to endanger an employee's sense of psychological safety. Low-context communicators prefer explicit and direct communication. In these cultures, being candid is highly valued (Hall, 1959). In contrast, high-context communicators look toward the surroundings of the interaction and emphasize relationship-building and saving face. In high-context oriented cultures, a direct callout about deadlines or mistakes may threaten face, especially when delivered by a manager. Instead, high-quality team-based interventions "where team members remind each other of deadlines and deliverables and clarify expectations with their teammates rather than outsiders or management" are key ways to ensure that all team members feel comfortable expressing their ideas and opinions (Fleischmann et al., 2023, p. 371). Similarly, virtual nudges, which don't necessarily come directly from a person, place information, such as a team's deadlines and task criteria, in front of an employee but with much lower stakes in terms of honor or confrontation. GVTs can struggle with planning and coordination because of time zone and cultural differences so virtual nudges can place deadlines and task details to the attention of each team member without it looking like a command or a reprimand. Such strategies are important tactics colleagues can use to ensure psychological safety and clear and effective exchange among team members.

Monochronic/Polychronic Dimension

The monochronic/polychronic dimension refers to the degree to which people compartmentalize and measure time. A strong orientation toward polychronism is often explained as the ability to do or process many things at once. In the polychronic view, time is important, but it is not necessarily linear or ordinal, especially for important tasks or personal interactions. Those at the polychronic end of the continuum will also comfortably interweave social, political, familial, and professional contexts, and feel little urge to end or finish meetings, decisions, or interactions. People with strong monochronic orientations generally do one thing at a time. They see the clock and the schedule as the structures by which to arrange their lives. Individuals with a monochronic perspective will measure success in an interaction if it has come to a firm and clear conclusion and in the process are likely to interrupt whatever they are doing, to "be on time" for a commitment.

Mastery/Adaptive Dimension

The final worldview dimension we will address is the mastery/adaptive dimension, which highlights humans' relationship with the natural world. As more and more nations and organizations prioritize environmental goals, critically examining this dimension is becoming increasingly important. The mastery view of nature assumes that humans can and should control the natural world. One way this worldview is performed is through ownership of natural resources such as land, water, and animals. Cultures with strong orientations toward mastering nature try to shape the environment with technology to make the natural world easier or more pleasing to humans (e.g., air conditioning, vehicles, genetic modification of food, electricity). At the other end of the spectrum are cultures that take an adaptive or harmonious attitude toward the world around them. Cultures with this perspective see humans not as owners but as partners with the natural world. They adapt and blend into their environment and often perform this worldview by building noninvasive architecture or harvesting resources based on a cycle of regrowth.

Recalling Figure 1.1, worldview orientations are reflected in a group's values and norms and codes, but the repetition of the values, norms, and codes reflects and reinfluences the greater ideology of the cultural system. The more cultural members hear a word or see a behavior that reinforces the dominant worldview and value system, the stronger their commitment to that worldview and value system. At the same time, cultural change happens at the level of codes and norms. If cultural members begin to talk or act in ways that contradict or devalue conventional values and worldview orientations, then those values and cultural positions on the continuum will also begin to shift.

Cross-Cultural Professional Interactions

Professionals learn values, norms, and codes predominantly within the national cultures where they received their educations and take their first jobs. Professionals are socialized into disciplinary and organizational systems that work much like regional or co-cultures (Hanges & Dickson, 2004; House et al., 2004; Mathison & Berkland, 2019). In many ways, the ideology or worldview of the national culture in which a professional's organization or discipline is embedded greatly influences professional norms and values (Warren & Lee, 2020). For example, such norms as "job hopping" may not be as common in a culture that is strongly collectivist leaning, as employees have much more loyalty to their groups and organizations. Similarly, executive pay may be closer to employee pay in egalitarian leaning cultures but vastly different in hierarchically leaning ones.

At a level of ideology, the national culture's worldview orientations impact the relationships among organizational structures, employee processes and priorities and the role employees and organizations serve in society (Karjalainen, 2020; Lauring, 2011). Assumptions and values are the deeper and less visible aspects of organizational and professional or disciplinary culture (Glisson & James, 2002; Schein, 1992) and cannot be directly observed but only analyzed by observing the behavior or communication of the group members (Hofstede, 1998). More apparent are the group's norms and codes (Glisson & James, 2002; Hofstede, 1998). Norms comprise the behaviors, rituals, and patterns that typify the professional group, such as meeting schedules and agendas, work group socialization, and the typical rules of workflow. Codes are the direct messages, slogans, sayings, or vocabulary that members of a professional group use to demonstrate their knowledge and competency. These norms and codes reflect the values and fundamental assumptions of the professional group but have some flexibility and can be changed as a result of interactions that alter or contradict the less visible aspects of culture.

Professional newcomers are taught cultural values and norms via the processes of educational and organizational socialization (see Kramer, 2010; Warren 2020), just as in broader or national cultures, interactions with organizational leaders and peers teach new members how to act appropriately within the specific context (Karahanna et al., 2005). The overlapping of ideological systems and worldviews within professional groups, and their associated values, norms, and codes can make it difficult to tease out the elements of social conditioning at one level of culture over another (Dickson et al., 2001; Mathison & Berkland, 2019). Where national culture ends and professional or organizational culture begins is impossible to determine. Complicating this puzzle is that professional subcultures vary within national systems and national systems contain diversity as well (Martin, 1992, 2002).

Business professionals in cross-cultural organizational interactions need to be attentive not only to the unique ideological manifestations of the national and co-cultures in which they find themselves (such as the United States, the U.S. South, or the Netherlands and its Groningen province), but to the way that professional norms work or interpret national structures (Griffith, 2002; Warren, 2020). By considering examples from across the globe and in different business contexts, our hope is that young and seasoned business professionals alike might learn to hone their ability to pay attention to these cultural nuances.

Overview of the Volume

Using Hoefstede's cultural orientations as a framework, the forthcoming chapters reveal how culture is discernable across a variety of interpersonal, organizational, and institutional business contexts. Together they demonstrate that the way cultures perceive and respond to professional situations is saturated by the values and ideologies of their national cultures. Written by international scholars from a variety of disciplines including communication, accounting, psychology, economics, public administration, and linguistics, each chapter provides a cultural comparison within a professional context. The contributions represent different cultures and different business sectors, and most are based on original empirical studies that undergird the practical orientation of this book. This multicultural volume features studies of Argentina, China, Germany, India, Japan, Morocco, the Netherlands, Norway, Poland, South Korea, the United Kingdom, and the United States, providing students a glimpse of how cultures infuse business practices across the globe. Together the chapters reveal how culture is discernable across a variety of business functions. Collectively, they underscore the need to cultivate cultural competency in professionals across the entire enterprise.

From human resource-focused questions such as how enthusiasm is communicated via words and smiles during the hiring process to how company loyalty is interpreted, national cultural values clearly infuse all kinds of professional interactions. Similarly, how store merchants organize their products tells us more about the expected norms for the interaction than the type or worth of the merchandise. Perhaps more surprising is how larger systems of currency exchange and financial reporting may also display cultural influences. These chapters demonstrate that the way cultures perceive and respond to professional situations is saturated by the values and ideologies of their national cultures. Business professionals who can identify, understand, and appreciate these cross-cultural orientations will be better equipped to navigate professional interactions in a global world (Warren, 2020).

The chapters in this volume are organized by scope into three levels: interpersonal interaction, group and organizational practices, and finally interorganizational and institutional practices. By showcasing a variety of practices from the micro level to the macro level, we show how culture permeates business interactions throughout, between, and beyond organizations.

At the interpersonal level, the chapters explore nonverbal, conversational, and mediated communication. In Chapter 2, Lao and Bencharit demonstrate how culturally based norms of emotional display influence hiring managers' decisions regarding potential employees. Zhu explains in Chapter 3 how cultural values imbue conversational turn-taking while talking in pairs and groups. Even in informal conversation, the potential for miscommunication is ripe because of the desire to show connection via interruptions or respect by refraining from interruption may be at odds. The way politeness is communicated via acknowledgment of hierarchy is another area of potential unintentional offense. In Chapter 4, Moon explains the way ideologies of value, particularly hierarchy/egalitarianism, manifests in professional communication by some cultural communicators. Their absence when expected could be considered disrespectful, but not every cultural system expects them.

At the group and organizational level, the chapters investigate how interactions among coworkers, supervisors-subordinates, and colleagues operationalize the abstract values of trust, loyalty, and respect in culturally distinctive ways. In Chapter 5, Nishishiba speaks to the cultural tension between individual value and group identity, and how it may cause employees to look for different traits in their coworkers. In their study of employee loyalty and work overload, Meschke and Du explain in Chapter 6 the distinct cultural differences between national cultures in terms of how employees perceive their supervisors and how, in turn, that relates to organizational loyalty and commitment. In Chapter 7, Buxbaum and Berkland examine a unique workplace in the Netherlands where a team of employees from diverse national cultural backgrounds responds to allegations of sexual harassment. Their formal response to organizational statements illustrates the ways multinational employee teams can harness the organizational and national values of their company to advocate for change.

Moving beyond the organization per se, the last set of studies show how cultures intersect and adapt to the presence of cultural outsiders, local conditions, and international standards. Chapter 8 explores how global tourism presents moments of unique cross-cultural interaction in retail spaces. Berkland argues that the one-sided nature of souvenir or artifact sales has a distinct power imbalance that can allow for immediate and long-lasting cultural drift. Mason and Dasgupta provide a cultural perspective on economic activity in Chapter 9, where we can see how cash is a tool used within culture to navigate tolerance to uncertainty and risk. Each national culture, however, has a different ability to mentally withstand and adapt to risk, illustrating the very human and cultural impact on the banking industry. In Chapter 10, Koleśnik and Silska-Gembka examine the norms and values that emerge *after* global professional standards are set and raise questions about cultural convergence. Finally, in the concluding chapter (Chapter 11), we reflect on the larger processes of cultural change and influence so that we might better appreciate what is potentially at stake whenever we engage in intercultural business communication.

Each of these chapters demonstrates a unique aspect of cross-cultural interaction that is unique to professional contexts. Many of these experiences, especially those dealing with decisions about finances or employment, are presumed to be based on objective, measurable criteria, when, in fact, they are as influenced by cultural values as handshakes, negotiations, and team bonding activities are. Global professionals, despite any attempts to be open and aware, carry with them their national, organizational, and disciplinary socializations, and bring those expectations to interactions. Understanding the context that a professional comes from is key to developing effective professional relationships across cultures.

References

Dickson, M. W., Smith, D. B., Grojean, M. W., & Ehrhart, M. (2001). An organizational climate regarding ethics: The outcome of leader values and the practices that reflect them. *The Leadership Quarterly, 12*(2), 197–217.

Fleischmann, C., Seeber, I., Cardon, P., & Aritz, J. (2023). Fostering psychological safety in global virtual teams: The role of digital reminder nudges and team-based interventions. *Proceedings of the 56th Hawaii International Conference on System Sciences.* https://hdl.handle.net/10125/102673

Geertz, C. (1973). *The interpretation of cultures.* New York: Basic Books.

Glisson, C., & James, L. R. (2002). The cross-level effects of culture and climate in human service teams. *Journal of Organizational Behavior, 23*(6), 767–794.

Griffith, D. A. (2002). The role of communication competencies in international business relationship development. *Journal of World Business, 37*, 256–265.

Hall, B. J., Covarrubias, P. O., & Kirschbaum, K. A. (2017). *Among cultures: The challenge of communication.* Milton Park: Routledge.

Hall, E. (1959). *The silent language.* New York: Doubleday.

Hanges, P. J., & Dickson, M. W. (2004). The development and validation of the GLOBE culture and leadership scales. In R. J. House, P. J. Hanges, M. Javidan, P. W. Dorfman, & V. Gupta (Eds.), *Leadership, culture, and organizations: The GLOBE study of 62 societies* (pp. 122–151). Thousand Oaks, CA: Sage.

Hofstede, G. (1980). Culture and organizations. *International Studies of Management & Organization, 10*(4), 15–41. https://doi.org/10.1080/00208825.1980.11656300

Hofstede, G. (1991). *Cultures and organizations: Software of the mind.* London, England: McGraw-Hill.

Hofstede, G. (1998). Attitudes, values and organizational culture: Disentangling the concepts. *Organization Studies, 19*(3), 477–493. https://doi.org/10.1177/017084069801900305

House, R. J., Hanges, P. J., Javidan, M., Dorfman, P. W., & Gupta, V. (Eds.). (2004). *Leadership, culture, and organizations: The GLOBE study of 62 societies.* Thousand Oaks, CA: Sage.

Karahanna, E., Evaristo, J. R., & Srite, M. (2005). Levels of culture and individual behavior: An investigative perspective. *Journal of Global Information Management (JGIM), 13*(2), 1–20.

Karjalainen, H. (2020). Cultural identity and its impact on today's multicultural organizations. *International Journal of Cross Cultural Management, 20*(2), 249–262.

Kramer, M. W. (2010). *Organizational socialization: Joining and leaving organizations.* Malden, MA: Polity Press.

Lauring, J. (2011). Intercultural organizational communication: The social organizing of interaction in international encounters. *The Journal of Business Communication (1973), 48*(3), 231–255.

Lian, H., Ferris, D. L., & Brown, D. J. (2012). Does power distance exacerbate or mitigate the effects of abusive supervision? It depends on the outcome. *Journal of Applied Psychology, 97*(1), 107–123.

Lindorff, M. (2010). The personal values of tomorrow's workforce: Similarities and differences across sex and nationality. *Journal of Management & Organization, 16*(3), 353–368. https://doi.org/10.5172/jmo.16.3.353

Martin, J. (1992). *Cultures in organizations: Three perspectives.* New York: Oxford University Press.

Martin, J. (2002). *Organizational culture: Mapping the terrain.* Thousand Oaks, CA: Sage.

Mathison, M., & Berkland, M. (2019). Creating cultural awareness in interdisciplinary programs. In M. Mathison (Ed.), *Sojourning in disciplinary cultures: A case study of teaching and writing in engineering.* Logan: Utah State University Press.

Salin, D., Cowan, R., Adewumi, O., Apospori, E., Bochantin, J., D'Cruz, P., ... Zedlacher, E. (2019). Workplace bullying across the globe: A cross-cultural comparison. *Personnel Review, 48*(1), 204–219.

Schein, E. (1992). *Organizational culture and leadership*. San Fransisco, CA: Jossey-Bass.
Warren, M., & Lee, W. (2020). Intercultural communication in professional and workplace settings. In J. Jackson (Ed.), *The Routledge handbook of language and intercultural communication* (pp. 473–486). Milton Park: Routledge.

PART 1
Interpersonal Contexts

2
CULTURAL DIFFERENCES IN THE DISPLAY OF EMOTION DURING THE HIRING PROCESS[1]

Chi Cheng Lao and Lucy Zhang Bencharit

As the world becomes more diverse, there is a call to match that demographic diversity in the workplace. As a response to this call-to-action, many companies have implemented a number of initiatives, including mandatory diversity training and education, as well as charges to increase numeric representation in hiring and promotions (Portocarrero & Carter, 2022). Despite these initiatives, vast underrepresentation remains, in particular for women and people of color across all sectors of the workplace. This leads to the question: how do we increase diversity in the workplace?

When addressing disparities in the workplace, much effort has focused on overt discrimination or employers' unconscious bias such as bias towards an individual's race, ethnicity, gender, and sex. One way that unconscious bias presents itself is through an employer's selection of job applicants. For example, Asian Americans whose names and experiences were "Whitened" were twice as likely to be interviewed by potential employers than those who kept their ethnic names and experiences (Kang et al., 2016). Another study of top-tier U.S. banking, law firms, and management consulting firms shows that many hiring evaluators prioritize their "gut" feelings and "cultural fit" (e.g., hobbies, background, and self-presentation styles) over the experiences and education of the candidates (Rivera, 2015). By using "cultural fit" as a criterion, employers are more likely to hire employees that are similar to themselves and homogenous to each other in racial and gender identification; thus, hiring based on such measures can lead to discrimination.

Another example comes from a series of studies that examined the effect of categorizing job candidates' résumés based on certain characteristics

DOI: 10.4324/9781003298199-4

(i.e., gender, nationality, universities). In different samples of Singaporean Chinese university students and human resource professionals, they found that separating candidates' résumés based on gender or nationality increased the likelihood of selecting a diverse pool of candidates (Feng et al., 2020). Moreover, the same study found that when choosing candidates based on résumés that are separated by gender (i.e., male or female), Singaporean students who have weaker stereotypes about engineering are more likely to choose women, whereas those who hold stronger stereotypes were unaffected by the categorization.

Based on these examples, we know that we can increase diversity and reduce discrimination by examining our hiring practices and evaluating how unconscious bias may creep into these processes. Next, we will delve deeper into one area where this is particularly important in the workplace: the display of emotions during the hiring process.

Emotions in Work Settings

Emotions play an important part in work settings, specifically how employees experience and regulate feelings at work. The way employees feel at work can impact their overall health and work outcomes. For instance, if people experience negative emotions at work and suppress them, they are more likely to have worse physical and mental health outcomes (Cybulska et al., 2022; Kshtriya et al., 2022). In addition, professions that are high in emotional labor (e.g., flight attendants, customer service workers) experience increased turnover due to employee burnout and emotional exhaustion (Hochschild, 1983). To reduce these effects and improve employee satisfaction and performance, companies could try enhancing the experience and expression of positive emotions (Wright & Cropanzano, 2000).

Although there is a wealth of literature examining the role of emotions in work settings, not enough research has examined emotion in the context of employment hiring, that is, when people are applying for a job or employers are hiring someone for a job. We propose that emotional expression can be a possible cue employers use – consciously or unconsciously – when choosing candidates to interview or hire.

Cultures vary in the emotions that they value and express. For instance, there are cross-cultural differences in the emotions that are valued in Western countries (e.g., the U.S. and much of Europe), where people tend to be more independent, and non-Western countries (e.g., Japan, China, and India), where people tend to be more interdependent. Next, we will review the research on how these cultural differences in emotions impact employment outcomes.

Affect Valuation Theory

Culture shapes our thoughts and behaviors in unique ways and certainly influences the way we perceive and express emotions. To help us understand emotions in the workplace better, we will review affect valuation theory (AVT; Tsai, 2017).

AVT proposes that:

1 there is a difference between people's actual emotions (i.e., the emotions they experience) and ideal emotions (i.e., the emotions they want to feel),
2 culture influences our ideal emotions more than actual emotions, and
3 our ideal emotions influence our daily lives.

Emotions are the feeling states that vary along the dimensions of valence (from negative to positive) and arousal (from low to high). There are many domains of people's emotional lives, including emotions of experience as well of desire. Ideal emotion describes the emotions that people value and ideally want to feel. It is a desired state that helps people interpret their own and others' emotional experiences ("How should I feel about this?"). For example, a person may want to feel excited and consequently decide to go to an amusement park. On the other hand, actual emotion describes the emotions people actually feel. It is how someone responds to an event or how they respond on average ("How do I feel now? How do I typically feel?"). For example, a person may feel relaxed when riding the merry-go-round at the amusement park.

As noted, emotions vary along dimensions of valence and arousal, and this chapter will focus on excitement states (high arousal positive (HAP) states) and calm states (low arousal positive (LAP) states). Excitement states include emotions such as excitement, enthusiasm, and elation. That could mean high-intensity smiles with teeth showing when thinking about facial expression. On the other hand, calm states include emotions such as calm, peacefulness, and relaxation, as exhibited by closed-mouth smiles. It is important to note that feeling calm does not mean there is no facial expression. It simply means that the smile is lower in intensity when compared to an excited smile.

Across cultures, emotional expressions that match the emotions someone values increase judgment of warmth and affiliation (Tsai et al., 2019). This is especially important because, across cultures, people are better at recognizing emotions from their own cultural groups (Elfenbein & Ambady, 2002), and that cultures differ in the emotions they ideally want to feel and value

(Tsai, Knutson, & Fung, 2006). In the same way that employers are more drawn to applicants with culturally normative names, employers may be more drawn to applicants whose emotions align with the emotions the employer and culture value. Thus, we can use AVT to start to unpack the intricate relationship between emotions and employment settings across cultures.

Specifically, research has focused on the cultural differences between groups in their valuation of excitement states and calm states. We have learned that European Americans tend to value excitement states more and calm states less than East Asian groups. East Asians, in contrast, tend to value calm states more than European Americans.

Emotional Diversity in Hiring

The role of ideal emotion in employment settings is a particularly interesting area because job applications and interviews are the gateways to the professional world. Indeed, the application process is often a place where people want to put their best selves forward. They are actively trying to demonstrate their knowledge and personality in a way that will attract employers. At the same time, employers are searching for the qualities they feel best fit the organization. Therefore, people's conceptions of ideal emotions in employment settings apply to both prospective employees and potential employers. Next, we will outline the research that shows whether cultural differences in ideal emotion play a role in how applicants present themselves when applying for a job and who people hire for jobs. In addition, we will look at what the implications of these differences are for increasing diversity in the workplace.

Cultural Contexts

In Western countries such as the U.S., individuals tend to value independence, while non-Western – particularly East Asian – countries tend to value interdependence. In a metanalysis of several different studies, researchers found that European Americans value independence more and interdependence less (Oyserman, Coon, & Kemmelmeier, 2002). On the other hand, Chinese showed less preference for independence and more for interdependence. These differences in independence and interdependence influence a host of emotional elements.

First, independence and interdependence can influence how much people strive for positive and negative emotional states. Indeed, European Americans prefer to maximize their positive emotions and minimize their negative emotions, rather than letting the two emotions exist at the same time (Miyamoto, Ma, & Wilken, 2017). In contrast, East Asians adopt a more balanced perspective between positive and negative emotions and may even view negative emotions as useful under stressful situations (Yoo et al., 2022). The way someone values positive versus negative emotions will certainly reflect their presentation in a job interview, which can often be stressful.

Second, independence and interdependence can influence how much people associate interpersonally engaging or disengaging emotions with positive feelings, like being happy. For example, European Americans associate positive feelings with interpersonally disengaging states, like pride. In contrast, Japanese associate positive feelings with interpersonally engaging emotions, like respect. One reason we see these differences is because Western cultures value standing out from others in a positive way, whereas Eastern cultures value fitting in with others (Kitayama, Markus, & Kurokawa, 2000). As we continue to read about emotions in the workplace, we will see how the preference for self-focused positive emotions is presented in the candidates' written responses to a job application.

Third, independence and interdependence can influence how much people value excitement states and calm states. This is what we focus on in the present chapter.

In reviewing the research on cultural differences in emotions, it is important to note that not a lot of research has examined the differences between East Asians and Asian Americans. Rather, the two groups unfortunately tend to be lumped together. Asian Americans are in a unique position where they learn and balance two cultures simultaneously. As such, we propose that their emotional values and expressions lie somewhere on a continuum between European Americans and East Asians. Consequently, this chapter compares the ideal emotions and values of three cultures: European Americans, Asian Americans, and Hong Kong (HK) Chinese.

Cultural Interaction: The Job Application Process

During the job application process, applicants need a résumé or CV, perhaps a cover letter, and will hopefully be invited for an interview. Ideal emotions, or the emotions that a person hopes to convey, will be present in all these products. However, there are cultural differences in how people present themselves in the workplace. Those differences are particularly visible through the words they use that convey their emotional state and the intensity of their smiles in their interactions.

Written Responses

As described in this chapter, European Americans use more excitement words than Asian Americans and HK Chinese. Table 2.1 lists word stems for excited/HAP states (left) and calm/LAP states (right).

Examples of responses to "Additional information about you" open-ended job application question

TABLE 2.1 Examples of word stems indicating excited or calm states

Excited *HAP States*	*Calm* *LAP States*
cheerf*	calm*
daring	carefree
elated	comfort*
energ*	ease*
enthus*	harmony
exhilar*	relax
inspir*	rest
jubilant	seren*
passion*	tranquil*

TABLE 2.2 Examples of written responses indicating excited and calm emotions

European American	*HK Chinese*
I am very interested in your company. I hope you give my application strong consideration.	I like challenges. I think Business Development Department is the place where I can discover and utilize my potential to the most and I am more than willing to rise to the challenge.
I am very excited for this opportunity and look forward to speaking with you.	I am fond of yoga and I have certificate on piano and electronic board, also I do volunteering work to Guizhou to help local primary school.
I am particularly excited about the opportunity to apply for an internship…because I find that the company's business values resonate with my own. I truly believe in the goals of the company, and it would be my honor to assist in any way that I could. Although I do have a little bit of experience, I am eager to learn and take on new tasks as the company needs. Thank you so much for your time and consideration.	In my spare time, I prefer to work as a volunteer to help others. That's why I love the job which serves people.

The differences in ideal emotions within written materials are reflected in the type of word used (Bencharit et al., 2019). European Americans used more words that conveyed excitement states than HK Chinese did, with Asian Americans falling in between the two. For instance, to express excitement in word form (see the left side of Table 2.1), an applicant may choose to include words such as "excited" or "passionate" in their application (see the left side of Table 2.2). While an applicant may choose to use words that indicate excitement because that particular state is the ideal emotion they want to convey, there is no evidence that differences in word use are due to the emotions the culture values.

On the other end of the spectrum are words that convey calm states. These (see the right side of Table 2.1) include words such as "ease" or "harmony." In the written response example, HK Chinese participants may not directly use words as in the ones listed in Table 2.1, but they convey the ideas expressed in these words (see the right side of Table 2.2).

Physical Expression of Emotions

The interview portion includes both verbal and nonverbal expressions and the key cultural differences manifest in the intensity of the candidates' smiles. The intensity of smiles are attempts to indicate the communicator's emotional state and are often the easiest nonverbal signal to identify. It is especially important to realize that individuals are better at recognizing emotions from their own cultural groups (Elfenbein & Ambady, 2002).

FIGURE 2.1 Differences in smile intensity between European American (left) and HK Chinese (right)

Photo credit: Lucy Zhang Bencharit.

In European American cultures, applicants tend to show smiles that are more pronounced, extreme, or maximal (see the left side of Figure 2.1). Those who show a high-intensity smile are "excited applicants." However, like the type of words used, the occurrence of high-intensity smiles is not predicted by the emotion but the cultural values. On the other hand, applicants in HK Chinese cultures show smiles that are more trace or slight (see the right side of Figure 2.1). Candidates who show a lower intensity of smile are "calm applicants." In recorded introductions of job interviews, European Americans showed more high-intensity smiles. Within HK Chinese, they showed calmer smiles.

Analysis

In the sample job materials, individuals signaled different emotions when communicating about themselves. Specifically, the emotions they wanted to convey in their job applications, the words they used in their applications to describe themselves and their experiences, and the smiles they displayed when they greeted potential interviewers varied based on their cultures of origin. Similarly, hiring managers show preferences for the emotions that candidates display and the candidates who most closely reflect their cultural expectations are subsequently hired.

Using the framework of AVT, the variability in emotional expressions during job interviews and preferences in hiring decisions is a direct result of our culturally shaped emotional values. In the U.S., we value, express, and look for excitement in others. While in other cultural contexts, like HK, we are more likely to value, express, and look for calmness in others. We see these differences in a number of situations (e.g., physician choice, interpersonal relationships), and the present work shows that they also manifest in employment settings.

Writing Emotions in Résumés

The first point of contact an employer has with an applicant is through the résumé and employers start forming impressions of candidates. On top of scanning experiences that fit the job position, employers are most likely scanning keywords that signal the applicant possesses a certain aura that fits the organization's culture.

European Americans viewed the ideal applicant as someone with a HAP state (excitement) who expresses more excitement states than HK Chinese, while HK Chinese viewed the ideal applicant as someone who expresses LAP state (calm) with calm-reflecting words. Asian Americans fell in between the two groups (Bencharit et al., 2019). More importantly, the more someone values excitement states, the more they will rate the ideal applicant as someone who expresses excitement states. There is a similar trend for those who value calm states, and this trend works above and beyond the effects of cultural groups. As a result, an employer's ideal emotion plays a big role in how they rate an applicant's written response and introduction.

The culture to which the company belongs and the cultural group with which the employer may identify influence the evaluation of cover letters and other written documents, and cultural similarity increases a candidate's chances of being selected for an interview. For instance, applicants applying for jobs at a company within the U.S. would benefit from including more words that signal excitement states such as excited, passionate, and interested. Words that convey an excitement state may reflect positive emotions that are more self-focused and thus an emotional state that reflects independence. In contrast, when applying for a company whose cultural orientation is geared towards HK Chinese culture, the applicant would be better served expressing a calm state with words like harmony, calm, and relaxed. Similarly, some of these words may reflect a candidate's value on interdependence. For instance, "harmony" suggests a candidate's priority for group achievement rather than individual achievement.

Signaling Emotions in Interviews

Emotional expectations are similarly continued through the interview process. Variables like tone, mouth position, eye movement, and posture are all examined from the perspective of the emotional state of the candidate. It turns out, when working adults with advanced training in business (i.e., MBA) and employees at a midsized company in the U.S. were asked to rate the likelihood of hiring an applicant, European Americans were more likely to hire the excited applicant (see Figure 2.2) than HK Chinese.

Expressing calm or excitement is important because of the values and dispositions that cultures prioritize in their workplaces. European Americans may value excitement more because the applicant's excitement transfers well for dealing with customers. Words like *interested* or *passionate* and expressions like wide, toothy smiles tell customers or colleagues that they are engaged. However, that sentiment often does not resonate with HK Chinese working adults in the same way. HK Chinese often see the excited applicant as insincere or unreliable.

On the other hand, when European Americans view the calm applicant, they often feel that the candidate is not as engaged or interested. The calm applicant may be seen as lacking self-focus and independence; therefore,

FIGURE 2.2 Facial expressions showing excited, calm, and neutral states

Photo credit: Lucy Zhang Bencharit.

European Americans may assume the candidate will not put much effort into their work. In comparison, HK Chinese see the calm candidate as more mature or flexible. This flexibility may signal to HK Chinese employers that the calm applicants also share similar values of interdependence, valuing the team over the self.

The Hiring Decision

Emotional states influence the likelihood a candidate will be hired. Reflecting the patterns already noted, preferences for excitement over calm or vice versa are based on cultural background (Bencharit et al., 2019). An applicant may want to lean towards conveying a calm emotional state in the presence of an employer or company with a Chinese background. This could mean having more "calm" emotion words, a slight smile, slower and more melodic speech, and few head movements.

One key takeaway is that in an international setting, calm is the safest emotional expression to employ when engaged in the hiring process. In the U.S., an applicant can increase their chances with a European American employer or company if they express more excitement. However, excited emotional expression in an HK Chinese environment may put the candidate at risk of being passed over.

AVT and the Hiring Process

Emotions provide a lot of information about a person and about ourselves. They can be expressed through a variety of ways including but not limited to word choice, vocal tone, body language, and facial expression. Following the premises of AVT, the way we ideally want to feel differs from how we actually feel. Moreover, our cultures shape our ideal emotions more than our actual emotions, and that has a host of consequences (Tsai, 2017). This chapter examined the expression of excitement state on perception of hireability in a new light. We observed that depending on what emotions the culture values, emotion's influence on hireability differs, such that European Americans value excitement states (HAP) more and HK Chinese value calm states (LAP) more. This knowledge can be utilized for both personal adjustments and management to improve cultural diversity in the workplace. For instance, the context of the company gives applicants an idea whether to present themselves more passionately or calmly. In addition, organizations may reassess their hiring procedures and implement training that addresses unconscious bias, in particular about cultural values and emotional expression in the hiring process.

Conclusion

As hiring mangers use emotional cues to decide whom to hire, they may be unintentionally limiting the diversity of their workforce. Because employers may not be aware of the way their ideal emotions influence their judgments, they may view an applicant with different emotional values as unqualified rather than valuing different emotional states. While many organizations are hosting mandatory diversity training and are reevaluating retention and promotion efforts, the expression of emotions is another factor to consider during the hiring process, because people may be hiring those who are like themselves or who express emotions that hint at shared cultural values. As such, organizations can add training and education surrounding culture and emotion, specifically the unspoken cultural assumptions that are tied to emotional expression.

Discussion Questions

- What emotions are most important to be communicated in the job application process?
- What words in a written response to a job call might signal that the applicant values excitement or calm states?

- What emotions might a person try to express emotions in a face-to-face job interview and through what strategies would those emotions be expressed?
- When comparing excited versus calm applicants, what values are being contrasted?
- How can hiring professionals become aware of and check their assumptions about cultural expression during the hiring process?

Note

1 Thank you to Dr. Jeanne Tsai and the Culture and Emotion Lab and Culture Collaboratory at Stanford University and to the Culture, Diversity and Identity Lab at Cal Poly, SLO. Thank you to all the research assistants and students who have made this research possible, including Angela Choi, Morgan Fuller, Gabi Greenberg, Mallika Roy, Sophie Ye, Henry Young, Grace Boorstein, Shawn Estrada, and Michelle Peretz.

Suggestions for Further Reading

Conelly, S., & Ruark, G. (2010). Leadership style and activating potential moderators of the relationships among leader emotional displays and outcomes. *Leadership Quarterly, 21*, 745–764. https://doi.org/10.1016/j.leaqua.2010.07.005

Gee, B., & Peck, D. (2016). *The illusion of Asian success: Scant progress for minorities in cracking the glass ceiling from 2007-2015–Ascend leadership foundation.* https://www.ascendleadership.org/thought-leadership/the-illusion-of-asian-success-scant-progress-for-minorities-in-cracking-the-glass-ceiling-from-2007-2015

Gündemir, S., Carton, A. M., & Homan, A. C. (2019). The impact of organizational performance on the emergence of Asian American leaders. *Journal of Applied Psychology, 104*(1), 107–122. https://doi.org/10.1037/apl0000347

Markus, H. R., & Kitayama, S. (1998). The cultural psychology of personality. *Journal of Cross-Cultural Psychology, 29*(1), 63–87. https://doi.org/10.1177/0022022198291004

Tsai, J. L. (2007). Ideal affect: Cultural causes and behavioral consequences. *Perspectives on Psychological Science, 2*, 242–259. http://doi.org/10.1111/j.1745-6916.2007.00043.x

References

Bencharit, L. Z., Ho, Y. W., Fung, H. H., Yeung, D. Y., Stephens, N. M., Romero-Canyas, R., & Tsai, J. L. (2019). Should job applicants be excited or calm? The role of culture and ideal affect in employment settings. *Emotion, 19*(3), 377–401. https://doi.org/10.1037/emo0000444

Cybulska, A. M., Rachubińska, K., Stanisławska, M., Grochans, S., Cymbaluk-Płoska, A., & Gronchans, E. (2022). Analysis of factors related to mental health suppression of emotions, and personality influencing coping with stress among nurses. *International Journal of Environmental Research and Public Health, 19*(16), 1–16. https://doi.org/10.3390/ijerph19169777

Elfenbein, H. A., & Ambady, N. (2002). On the universality and cultural specificity of emotion recognition: A meta-analysis. *Psychological Bulletin, 128*, 203–235. http://doi.org/10.1037/0033-2909.128.2.203

Feng, Z., Liu, Y., Wang, Z., & Savani, K. (2020). Let's choose one of each: Using the partition dependence effect to increase diversity in organizations. *Organizational Behavior and Human Decision Processes, 158*, 11–26. https://doi.org/10.1016/j.obhdp.2020.01.011

Hochschild, A. R. (1983). *The managed heart: Commercialization of human feeling*. Los Angeles: University of California Press.

Kang, S. K., DeCelles, K. A., Tilcsik, A., & Jun, S. (2016). Whitened resumes: Race and self-presentation in the labor market. *Administrative Science Quarterly, 61*, 469–502. https://doi.org/10.1177/0001839216639577

Kitayama, S., Markus, H. R., & Kurokawa, M. (2000). Culture, emotion, and well-being: Good feelings in Japan and the United States. *Cognition and Emotion, 14*(1), 93–124. https://doi.org/10.1080/026999300379003

Kshtriya, S., Lawrence, J., Kobezak, H. M., Popok, P. J., & Lowe, S. (2022). Investigating strategies of emotion regulation as mediators of occupational stressors and mental health outcomes in first responders. *International Journal of Environmental Research and Public Health, 19*(12), 1–13. https://doi.org/10.3390/ijerph19127009

Miyamoto, Y., Ma, X., & Wilken, B. (2017). Cultural variation in pro-positive versus balanced systems of emotions. *Current Opinion in Behavioral Science, 15*, 27–32. https://doi.org/10.1016/j.cobeha.2017.05.014

Oyserman, D., Coon, H. M., & Kemmelmeier, M. (2002). Rethinking individualism and collectivism: Evaluation of theoretical assumptions and meta-analysis. *Psychological Bulletin, 128*, 3–72. https://doi.org/10.1037/0033-2909.128.1.3

Portocarrero, S., & Carter, J. T. (2022). Diversity initiatives in the US workplace: A brief history, their intended and unintended consequences. *Sociology Compass, 16*(7), 1–12. https://doi.org/10.1111/soc4.13001

Rivera, L. A. (2015). Go with your gut: Emotion and evaluation in job interviews. *American Journal of Sociology, 120*, 1339–1389. https://doi.org/10.1086/681214

Tsai, J. L. (2017). Ideal affect in daily life: Implications for affective experience, health, and social behavior. *Current Opinion in Psychology, 17*, 118–128. http://doi.org/10.1016/j.copsyc.2017.07.004

Tsai, J. L., Blevins, E., Bencharit, L. Z., Chim, L., Fung, H. H., & Yeung, D. Y. (2019). Cultural variation in social judgments of smiles: The role of ideal affect. *Journal of Personality and Social Psychology, 116*(6), 966–988. https://doi.org/10.1037/pspp0000192

Tsai, J. L., Knutson, B., & Fung, H. H. (2006). Cultural variation in affect valuation. *Journal of Personality and Social Psychology, 90*, 288–307. http://doi.org/10.1037/0022-3514.90.2.288

Wright, T. A., & Cropanzano, R. (2000). Psychological well-being and job satisfaction as predictors of job performance. *Journal of Occupational Health Psychology, 5*, 84–94. http://dx.doi.org/10.1037/1076-8998.5.1.84

Yoo, J., Martin, J., Niedenthal, P., & Miyamoto, Y. (2022). Valuation of emotion underlines cultural variation in cardiovascular stress responses. *Emotions, 22*(8), 1801–1814. https://doi.org/10.1037/emo0000964

3
CULTURAL NORMS OF TURN-TAKING IN ENGLISH AND CHINESE CONVERSATIONS

Weihua Zhu

Humans are social beings who conduct conversations with each other in various settings. A smooth conversation requires turn-taking protocol due to the difficulty of speaking and listening at the same time and the challenge of coordinating who speaks and who listens. This chapter aims to illustrate the relationship between turn-taking and context. It shows that the similarities and differences in turn-taking in English and Chinese conversations are constrained by various factors. The differences could lead to intercultural communication issues.

Turn-Taking in Conversations

Turn-taking refers to a change of speaker in ordinary conversation. Speakers tend to follow some turn-taking rules to organize their conversations and ensure smooth communication (Sacks, Schegloff & Jefferson, 1974).

A unit of speech called a turn construction unit (TCU) is a speaker's stretch of speech to which other people listen. The stretch of speech could be short or long, depending on when the speaker finishes their thoughts. At the end of this TCU is a transition relevance place (TRP). At this place, the current speaker may select the next speaker, which is termed "other-select", by calling upon or looking at that person. If that does not occur, any other listener can gain the turn by starting to talk, which is termed "self-select". The use of the self-selection technique is contingent on the nonuse of the other-select technique. If neither other-select nor self-select transpires, the current speaker may continue. This is very similar to floor taking. When the current speaker has "the focus of attention of the ongoing topic" (Hayashi, 1991, p. 3), it means that they have the floor. The floor holder can select the next speaker or let others select themselves. If no one else wants to take the floor, the current speaker may keep it.

With the intention of keeping the floor, the current speaker might produce turn-holding cues such as "uh" or "um" (Ball, 1975), level intonation, or hand movement away from the body (Duncan, 1972) at non-TRPs. The turn-holding cues tend to successfully prevent listeners from initiating a new turn if they follow certain norms of interaction. When the current speaker is ready to give up the turn, they might deploy turn-yielding cues at TRPs. These cues are embedded in intonation, paralanguage, body motion, content, or syntax (Duncan, 1974). For example, ending a sentence with a falling tone or putting hands down could serve as signals for the next speaker to take over. It is common for the current speaker to provide multimodal cues such as "phrase-final intonation, termination of hand gesticulation, and completion of a grammatical clause" (Skantze, 2021, p. 4) to indicate the end of their turn.

The next speaker can also initiate signals showing their willingness to take over the turn. These signals are termed "turn-initial cues". They include "uh", "um" (Ball, 1975), gazing away, in-breath, or a gesture (Duncan, 1974) that is deployed before or at the beginning of a turn.

Turn-initial cues differ from backchannels such as "yeah", "mm-hmm", "uh-huh", head nods, and shakes, which are produced to demonstrate listeners' attentiveness or comprehension of the ongoing speech rather than taking a turn. In other words, backchannels are not considered turns in a conversation. They tend to emerge after the current speaker employs backchannel-inviting cues such as "you know?" or "right?" to engage listeners or check their understanding (Clark, 1996). Fortunately, in most cases, listeners do not attempt to grab the turn after producing backchannels, which allows the current speaker to continue the ongoing speech instead of yielding their turn.

Adjacency Pair

When a listener responds to the current speaker's invitation to join a conversation, it engenders an adjacency pair, which is a minimal version of turn-taking in a conversation (Sacks, Schegloff & Jefferson, 1974). An adjacency pair can be realized in diverse forms such as a question asked by one party and an answer provided by the other party, a greeting by one party and another greeting returned by the other party, an invitation by one party and acceptance by the other party, or a request by one party and refusal by the other party.

Overlapping

In some cases, without the current speaker's invitation, a listener may attempt to cut in rather than waiting for an invitation, which would result in a brief overlap, long overlap, or interruption (Sacks, Schegloff & Jefferson, 1974). Brief overlaps tend to occur at TRPs unintentionally. They include backchannels, terminal overlaps that occur when the listener begins speaking immediately before the speaker ends their turn, sentence completion when the listener helps the speaker complete their turn, and choral talk such as greetings or laughter (Schegloff, 2000). Although these brief overlaps are cooperative, they are still considered "errors and violations" (Sacks, Schegloff & Jefferson, 1974, p. 701) which, according to Schegloff (2000), should be resolved in fewer than three syllables from the first speaker's utterance completion place. This practice minimizes the emergence of long simultaneous speech at a TRP because long overlapping has been assumed to be problematic.

The concept of overlap differs from the concept of interruption. We can easily identify overlaps when hearing simultaneous speech. But interruptions can occur with or without overlapping speech. Interruption is more a subjective judgment (Bennett, 1981). When the current speaker feels that the next speaker violates their right to speak or when the next speaker cuts in and stops the current speaker from completing their thoughts, this behavior is considered interruption. Interruption is often deemed inappropriate and should be avoided especially in formal settings where following turn-taking rules is important for events to proceed smoothly.

Repair

Overlapping or interruption is often believed to violate typical turn-taking rules and cause communication breakdown. If overlapping or interruption prevents speakers from getting their message across, maintaining mutual understanding, or keeping their conversation flowing, they need to repair what they have said. Repair "operates in conversation to deal with problems in speaking, hearing, and understanding the talk in conversation" (Schegloff, Jefferson & Sacks, 1977, pp. 361–382). After locating the source of a problem, speakers can initiate repair and try to solve the problem. Repair can be started and finished by the speaker or others. Repair strategies include pausing within a turn, repeating what has been said with a rising tone, and asking for clarification about trouble sources (Sacks, Schegloff & Jefferson, 1974).

Cultural Contexts: American English and Mandarin Chinese

How people from distinct linguistic and cultural backgrounds communicate may differ from how they talk with people who share the same background. Not knowing the organization of conversations in American English and

Mandarin Chinese could cause misperceptions and misunderstandings in intercultural communication between American and Chinese people. Communication between people from these two different cultures runs the danger of being ineffective, and their interpretations of others' intentions incorrect, due to the assumption that people share the same linguistic rules. Undoubtedly, we should become aware of different conversational patterns outside of our comfort zone and learn how to communicate appropriately with people from another culture.

Generally speaking, turn-taking in a conversation is a culture-specific phenomenon. Turn-taking patterns can vary in different sociocultural and interactional contexts. By comparing turn-taking patterns in two different cultures/languages such as American English and Mandarin Chinese, we can see the effect of context on the use of language.

In a conversation in American English, it is typical that speakers alternate to ensure that one party speaks at a time although the number of speakers varies. Transitions occur smoothly at TRPs. Although brief overlaps do emerge occasionally, they should be terminated within three syllables of the current speaker's final words. The size and ordering of turns vary. The length and content of conversation are not predetermined except when it is in a formal meeting. Techniques are employed for turn allocation and repair (Sacks, Schegloff & Jefferson, 1974). Violations of these turn-taking mechanisms are deemed problematic and should be avoided (Schegloff, 2000).

Despite some similarities to turn-taking in American English (e.g., speaker alternation, variation in turn order, turn size, speaker number, unpredictability of conversation content, and turn-initial cues), turn-taking in Mandarin Chinese features long overlapping at a TRP. Long overlapping that is initiated by the next speaker more than three words from the current speaker's utterance completion place is called "extended concurrent speech" (Zhu, 2016, p. 638). Although extended concurrent speech transgresses Sacks, Schegloff, and Jefferson's (1974) orderly turn-taking rules and might be treated as competitive overlap, it can still serve positive functions, such as achieving relational goals (Zhu, 2016), clarifying things, and displaying active engagement (Zhu, 2017b), which contribute to an enjoyable interaction. Mandarin Chinese speakers can consider this type of long overlapping to be an appropriate, rather than problematic, communicative act (Zhu, 2017a).

Patterns of Turn-Taking in American English and Mandarin Chinese

To understand turn-taking patterns in American English and Mandarin Chinese, let us look at some excerpts from naturally occurring conversations among professionals in a Midwestern American city and a Southeastern Chinese city, respectively (Boxes 3.1–3.4).

BOX 3.1   AMERICAN ENGLISH—EXCERPT 1

Excerpt 1

In this excerpt, Daisy and Noey are female friends in their early 20s who are undergoing staff training at a university.
Excerpt 1 (Training)

1 Daisy: Did you only have one training session today?
2 Noey: I only have one session on Mondays, Wednesdays.
3 Daisy: You skipped your last session? Is it recorded though?
4 Noey: Yeah.
5 Daisy: Is that the one with the weird voice director?
6 Noey: See I only skipped the sessions more like they have audio or video.
7 Daisy: Yeah. They post the slides.
8 Noey: Yeah.
9 Daisy: No, that's fair.

BOX 3.2   AMERICAN ENGLISH—EXCERPT 2

Excerpt 2

In this excerpt, Yvonne is an elementary school teacher in her late 20s. Don is a technician in his 30s working for a company. They are acquaintances.
Excerpt 2 (Glue)

1 Yvonne: What's the weirdest thing you ever ate?
2 Don: Probably, something like glue when I was a kid.
    [(laughter)]
3 Yvonne: [Wait] a minute. That explains things, actually.
4 Don: I'm sure, [yes.]
5 Yvonne: [(laughter)] There's food all over this. Okay.
    (Background noise)
6 Yvonne: So, you had some glue.
7 Don: When I was in kindergarten, I'm sure I probably tried it.
8 Yvonne: Glue snacks, okay.

       [(laughter)]
9 Don: [Fruit] Roll-Up snack [with glue.]
10 Yvonne: [(laughter)]
11 Don: With dipping sauce.
12 Yvonne: Roll it up like a Hostess Cake?
       [(laughter)]
13 Don: [Yes.]

BOX 3.3   MANDARIN CHINESE CONVERSATION—EXCERPT 3

Excerpt 3

In this excerpt, Xiu and Jian graduated from the same university 15 years ago. They are female English teachers in a private college and a public university, respectively. They are friends.

Except 3 (LuXu6)

1 秀：我说干嘛花那么钱买一件那种衣服。我这人就是这样的。
2 剑：那是不是跟你的经济条件有关哪？就是说，你现在经济条件还宽裕了就[会这样。]
3 秀：[不是，不]是。跟小的时候花钱没有没有计划有关，从小没有培养好，因[为父母]
4 剑：[(laughter)还要]培养。
5 秀：对，因为我们小的时候手上没有钱，没有有钱的时候，父母就从来不会给你身上放钱。

(Translation)

1 Xiu: I said why you spent so much money on that dress. I'm just like that.
2 Jian: Does that have anything to do with your financial situation? I mean, you're better now. [That's why.]
3 Xiu: [No, no.] It has something to do with me spending money without a plan as a kid. I have no training in that aspect because [my parents]
4 Jian: [(laughter) You need] training.
5 Xiu: Yes, because we didn't have money when we were young. My parents never gave us pocket money.

> **BOX 3.4   MANDARIN CHINESE CONVERSATION—EXCERPT 4**
>
> **Excerpt 4**
>
> In this excerpt, Lian is a female college English teacher at a Chinese university. Jie is a female Ph.D. student of linguistics at a different university. They became acquainted through a common friend.
> Excerpt 4 (Nada)
>
> 1 廉：呃，[你教的学生是什么学生啊?]
> 2 杰：[对，　在那个学校的两个]
> 3 廉：你教的学生是什么学生啊?
> 4 杰：本科生，怎么可能是研究生呢?
> 5 廉：还是本科生。[他是属于什么样的学生?]
> 6 杰：[研究生是不能教研究生的。]
> 7 廉：哎，是外语专业的?
> 8 杰：不一定。
>
> (Translation)
>
> 1 Lian: Uh, [What type of students do you teach?]
> 2 Jie: [Yeah, at that school, the two]
> 3 Lian: What type of students do you teach?
> 4 Jie: Undergraduate students. How could it be graduate students?
> 5 Lian: Still undergrads. [What kind of undergrads?]
> 6 Jie: [Grads cannot teach grads.]
> 7 Lian: Ei, do they major in foreign language studies?
> 8 Jie: Not necessary.

Practice of Turn-Taking

A cross-culture and cross-language practice of turn-taking is to yield a turn by asking a question as the first part of an adjacency pair (e.g., Lines 1, 3, and 5 in Excerpt 1; Lines 1 and 12 in Excerpt 2; Line 2 in Excerpt 3; Lines 1, 3, 5, and 7 in Excerpt 4). Asking questions can actively engage listeners in a conversation and give them equal rights to express ideas. When the next speaker answers the question as the second part of the adjacency pair, they initiate a new turn. If the next speaker starts to respond within the three syllables of the first speaker's final word(s), a terminal overlap emerges (e.g., Lines 2, 3, and 4 in Excerpt 3). Brief overlaps also emerge frequently when the listener tries to demonstrate attentiveness and comprehension of the ongoing speech by producing backchannels (e.g., Line 8 in Excerpt 1; Line 13 in Excerpt 2) or laughter (e.g., Lines 2, 5, 8, 10, and 12 in Excerpt 2). But this type of overlapping tends to be resolved by one of the speakers ceasing talking so that whatever is being said can be heard clearly. This practice exists in both the American English and Mandarin Chinese conversations.

However, some turn-taking behavior might exist more in one culture or language than in another. For instance, long overlapping such as extended concurrent speech can be pinpointed in the Mandarin Chinese conversations (e.g., Lines 1, 2, 5, and 6 in Excerpt 4). Since extended concurrent speech in Mandarin Chinese can serve as a pragmatic strategy for high involvement (Tannen, 2007) or as a passionate contribution that helps maintain or enhance interpersonal relationships (Zhu, 2016), the Mandarin Chinese speakers might not perceive extended concurrent speech as inappropriate or problematic. They do not terminate it prematurely or repair it immediately. In contrast, extended concurrent speech does not appear in the American English conversations. This indicates that the American English speakers tend to abide by Sacks, Schegloff, and Jefferson's (1974) turn-taking rule of one speaker at a time.

Contextual Factors

Turn-taking is constrained by contextual factors that affect how closely people follow certain types of norms. It can be accounted for by Zhu's (2019) model of context, practice, and perception, as shown in Figure 3.1.

In this figure, we can see the interconnection among context, practice, and perception. The sociocultural context refers to a macro environment including temporality, the region, and the setting. The interactional context involves conversation-related factors such as interactional goals, risks, topics, relevance, verbal/nonverbal cues, social distance, and status differences. The personal context encompasses individual traits such as sex, age, education, temperament, habits, awareness, and beliefs. All of these contextual factors constrain how communicative acts are realized and perceived. Speakers' habitual practice of communicative acts can shape their perceptions of the (im)properness of verbal exchanges. In turn, these perceptions may influence their decisions on when, where, and how to verbally engage.

Take, for example, the turn-taking behavior in the American English conversations. The broad sociocultural context of the conversations is the contemporary United States, where linguistic forms and interactional norms can differ from what they were historically. The American English conversations took place in an apartment (Except 1) or coffee shop (Excerpt 2) in a Midwestern American city. The interactional context of the conversations

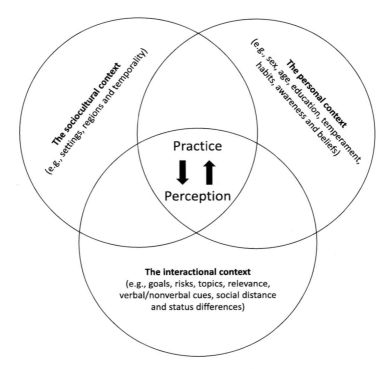

FIGURE 3.1 A model of context, practice, and perception (Zhu, 2019, p. 14)

includes the speakers' interactional goal of socializing with each other, the trivial and low-risk conversation topics such as training (Excerpt 1) and glue (Excerpt 2), the short social distance between the speakers, and minimal status difference between the speakers. What has been well known in terms of the speakers' personal contexts is their belief in cultural accommodation, a part of Midwestern distinctiveness (Cayton & Gray, 2001). They seek to compromise to maintain rapport in a cultural mix. This could explicate why the speakers repair overlapping and avoid interruptions in American English.

In contrast, the broad sociocultural context of the Mandarin Chinese conversations is mainland China that may feature different linguistic forms and interactional norms from Ancient China and contemporary United States. The Chinese conversations occurred in a condo (Excerpt 3) or a library (Excerpt 4) in a Southeastern Chinese city. All of the conversations occurred in informal settings, which might have made the speakers feel more comfortable taking turns as they habitually do. The interactional context of the conversations includes the speakers' interactional goal of socializing with each other, the trivial and low-risk conversation topics such as expenditure (Excerpt 3) and students (Excerpt 4), and little status difference between the speakers. The speakers were either friends (Excerpt 3) or acquaintances (Excerpt 4) and did not refrain from producing extended concurrent speech. This might be related to their personal context—their belief in high involvement and active engagement in conversations (Zhu, 2017a).

Conclusion

Although turn-taking in American English and Mandarin Chinese conversations shares some commonalities, such as using adjacency pairs, it varies due to macro and micro contextual factors such as regional culture and personal beliefs. Specifically, American English speakers are likely to repair overlapping turns because they tend to view overlapping as problematic and impolite, whereas Mandarin Chinese speakers do not mind talking simultaneously beyond the third syllable of their overlapped words because they are inclined to perceive overlapping as engaging and appropriate. Without this awareness, speakers from these two different cultures, when working together, might encounter communication breakdowns or misunderstandings, which can damage their relationship and thus inhibit their ability to work together effectively. To avoid miscommunication that might lead to negative consequences in professional settings, professionals must understand cross-cultural differences in the organization of turn-taking in conversations.

Discussion Questions

- What are some of the common turn-yielding cues and turn-initial cues in the American English and Mandarin Chinese conversations?
- How does overlapping in the American English conversations differ from that in the Mandarin Chinese conversations?
- How do the American English speakers differ from the Mandarin Chinese speakers in terms of repair strategies?
- What contextual factors might have influenced how the American English and Mandarin Chinese speakers took turns in those conversations?
- What are the potential communication problems that might result from the differences in overlapping and repair strategies between the American English speakers and the Mandarin Chinese speakers?

Suggestions for Further Reading

Duncan, S. (1974). On signaling that it's your turn to speak. *Journal of Experimental Social Psychology, 10*(3), 234–247.

Sacks, H., Schegloff, E., & Jefferson, G. (1974). A simplest systematics for the organization of turn-taking for conversation. *Language, 50*(4), 696–735.

Zhu, W. (2019). *Interaction in Mandarin Chinese and English as a multilingua franca: Context, practice, and perception.* Milton Park: Routledge.

References

Ball, P. (1975). Listeners' responses to filled pauses in relation to floor apportionment. *British Journal of Social & Clinical Psychology, 14*(4), 423–424.

Bennett, A. (1981). Interruptions and the interpretation of conversation. *Discourse Process, 4*, 171–188.

Cayton, A., & Gray, S. (Eds.). (2001). *The American Midwest: Essays on regional history.* Bloomington: Indiana University Press.

Clark, H. (1996). *Using language.* Cambridge: Cambridge University Press.

Duncan, S. (1972). Some signals and rules for taking speaking turns in conversations. *Journal of Personality and Social Psychology, 23*(2), 283. https://doi.org/10.1037/h0033031

Hayashi, R. (1991). Floor structure of English and Japanese conversation. *Journal of Pragmatics, 16*, 1–30.

Schegloff, E. A. (2000). Overlapping talk and the organization of turn-taking for conversation. *Language in Society, 29*(1), 1–63.

Schegloff, E. A., Jefferson, G., & Sacks, H. (1977). The performance for self-correction in the organization of repair in conversation. *Language, 53*, 361–382.

Skantze, G. (2021). Turn-taking in conversational systems and human-robot interaction: A review. *Computer Speech & Language, 67*, 101178.

Tannen, D. (2007). *Talking voices: Repetition, dialogue, and imagery in conversational discourse.* Cambridge: Cambridge University Press.

Zhu, W. (2016). Extended concurrent speech and *guānxì* management in Mandarin. *Text & Talk, 36*(5), 637–660.

Zhu, W. (2017a). Perceptions of extended concurrent speech in Mandarin. *Pragmatics, 27*(1), 145–171.

Zhu, W. (2017b). How do Chinese speakers of English manage rapport in extended concurrent speech? *Multilingua, 36*(2), 181–204.

4
CULTURAL VARIATIONS IN POLITENESS STRATEGIES USED IN EMAIL COMMUNICATION

Chanki Moon

"Being polite" can be considered one of the most important success strategies in the workplace as well as in personal interactions. Politeness enables individuals to save or support their face and the face of others (Brown & Levinson, 1987). The strategic use of polite expressions based on a universal concern to save or support the face of one's own and others may be the key to successful management of interpersonal communication in the workplace. However, cultural norms of politeness and communication styles can vary across cultures. By comparing examples of email communication in two different national cultures, this chapter explores the impact of cultural dimensions on politeness strategy.

Politeness as a Face-Saving Strategy in Interpersonal Communication

Politeness behavior is often understood in relation to the concept of face. *Face* was defined by Goffman (1967) as "the positive social value a person claims for him/herself" (p. 5). Face can be further divided into two types: positive and negative. *Positive face* refers to the positive self-image the individual wants to be approved and appreciated by others ('a desire for approval'), and *negative face* refers to the freedom from imposition or control by others ('a desire for autonomy'). Positive face can be threatened by certain behaviors such as social rejection/exclusion, criticism, and incivility/rudeness. Additionally, some behaviors such as seeking favors, giving orders, and making requests can threaten negative face (Goldsmith & Lamb Normand, 2015). In human interactions, people encounter various face-threatening acts. In response, people enact politeness strategies, or efforts to minimize face threat, when they communicate with others.

Culture and Communication Styles

Communication styles, defined as behaviors that occur consistently in the "way one verbally, nonverbally, and paraverbally interacts to signal how literal meaning should be taken, interpreted, filtered, or understood" (Norton, 1983, p. 58), can differ across cultures. So too can context, a term that reflects the rules for information sharing, vary among cultures (Gudykunst, 2001; Hall, 1976). Context influences how different values such as harmony, efficiency, clarity, or shame are prioritized.

Asian cultures tend to adhere to high-context communication styles through which "most of the information is either in the physical context or internalized in the person, while very little is in the coded, explicit, transmitted part of the message" (Hall, 1976, p. 79). In other words, in a high-context society, successful communication depends on how well messages between communicators are interpreted based on surrounding cues, historical information, and social expectations. One possible reason high-context communication is valued is the influence of Confucianism in East Asia. Confucian philosophy emphasizes harmony in interpersonal relationships. People in East Asia develop and maintain harmonious relationships with others through their communication, especially using indirect communication styles.

Indirect communication occurs when

> the speaker communicates to the hearer more than he [sic] actually says by way of relying on their mutually shared background information, both linguistic and non-linguistic, together with the general powers of rationality and inference on the part of the hearer.
>
> *(Searle, 1969, p. 60)*

Interestingly, in East Asia, the use of indirect communication may depend on the relational status between communicators; people tend to use more indirect communication styles when their interaction partner's status (e.g., age, position) is higher because the interaction partner's face can be saved. Indirect communication can be a strategic way to manage face-threatening situations in interpersonal interactions embedded in hierarchical organizational relationships.

In contrast, Western cultures tend to adhere to low-context communication styles in which the "mass of the information is vested in the explicit code" (Hall, 1976, p. 111). Communicators with low-context styles will state explicitly information that could be otherwise discerned for the sake of clarity and emphasis. Similarly, direct communication is preferred as accuracy and efficiency of interaction are more highly valued than harmony or saving a communication partner's face.

Collectivism (vs. Individualism), Face (vs. Dignity), and Power Distance

Some cultural dimensions are central to understanding cultural differences in communication styles. Since cultural differences may not be explained by a sole cultural dimension, we must consider the interconnectedness between cultural dimensions in order to understand communication styles and politeness strategies in interpersonal relationships, particularly hierarchical relationships. Three cultural dimensions are especially relevant: collectivism vs. individualism, face vs. dignity, and power distance.

Individualism can be seen in "societies in which the ties between individuals are loose: everyone is expected to look after him- or herself and his or her immediate family" (Hofstede, Hofstede, & Minkov, 2010, p. 92). In contrast, collectivism is related to the notion that the "societies in which people from birth onward are integrated into strong, cohesive in-groups, which throughout people's lifetime continue to protect them in exchange for unquestioned loyalty" (Hofstede, Hofstede, & Minkov, 2010, p. 92). The concept of collectivism characterized by relational interdependence is one of the clearest features in East Asian cultures. Collectivism may have originated from the cultural ethos of Confucianism which emphasizes values such as harmony, benevolence, compassion, and respect for authority. Confucianism also provides guidance for hierarchical interpersonal relationships (e.g., parent–offspring, elders–juniors, and ruler–subject). For instance, parent, elder, and ruler should treat others with mercy, kindness, and righteousness, and on the contrary, citizens and children must act with a sense of loyalty, respect, obedience, and filial piety (Zhong et al., 2006).

East Asians are also described as having *face culture* in which people's worth is largely defined by what other people think of them. A stable hierarchy is important in the context of face culture. The culturally specific concept of face was described as "the respectability and/or deference which a person can claim for himself [or herself] from others by virtue of [his or her] relative position" (Ho, 1976, p. 883) in a hierarchy and the proper fulfillment of his or her role. In contrast, Western countries are known as *dignity cultures* in which people's worth is not defined by other people's evaluation and equality is an important value. Dignity is "the conviction that each individual at birth possesses an intrinsic value at least theoretically equal to that of every other person" (Ayers, 1984, p. 19).

Finally, *power distance* is defined as the extent to which individuals accept inequality in society and/or in an organization (Hofstede, Hofstede, & Minkov, 2010). In high (vs. low) power-distance cultures, individuals tend to pay more attention to their communication partner's hierarchical status and regulate their communication style accordingly due to the collectivistic and hierarchical nature of their society (Moon et al., 2019). In low power-distance cultures, signifiers of rank are less frequent, with clear and direct communication prioritized.

Cultural Contexts: South Korea and the United Kingdom/the United States

Cultural norms and communication styles can vary across cultures. By comparing examples of email communication in two different national cultures (East Asia vs. Western), it is possible to see the impact of cultural dimensions on individual's communication styles as a politeness strategy.

The first national culture in this case is South Korea. South Korea's dominant cultural themes are collectivism, face, and high power distance. On the Individualism Distance Index (IDV), South Korea ranks 65 out of 76 countries and on the Power Distance Index (PDI; Hofstede, Hofstede, & Minkov, 2010), South Korea ranks 41–42, indicating that values of group harmony and respect for authority are emphasized. Furthermore, for Koreans living in a face society, it is important to evaluate themselves in relationship to others and any evaluation that places oneself above others is not considered modest. Hence, self-criticism may be more relevant than self-assessment/presentation. In order to understand Koreans' polite behavior in interpersonal communication, it is also necessary to consider the grammatical characteristics of Korean; the use of honorific language is a key feature for politeness in verbal communication.

The second national culture in this case includes both the United Kingdom and the United States. The United Kingdom/United States' dominant cultural themes are individualism, dignity, and low power distance. On the IDV, the United Kingdom ranks 3 and the United States 3 out of 76 countries, and on the PDI, the United Kingdom ranks 65–67 and the United States 59–62 (Hofstede, Hofstede, & Minkov, 2010), indicating that values of independence and uniqueness of self are highlighted. The United Kingdom and the United States are less hierarchically structured and the freedom of people to define themselves is important; self-assessment/presentation may be more common than self-criticism.

Cultural Differences in Politeness in Email Communication

Email is an important communication tool in workplaces across cultures, despite the lack of nonverbal cues compared to face-to-face communication. In a globalizing world, the importance of intercultural communication is becoming more prominent as many companies embrace internationalization.

In this sense, increasing cultural competence is required to manage interpersonal communication successfully. Intercultural communication is influenced by how context is used in culture, whether it is high or low context (Hall, 1976).

Indirect styles of communication are more dominant in high-context cultures compared with low-context cultures where people prefer direct communication styles and rely more on explicit information to interpret the meaning of messages. In addition, the level of formality in email communications is an important feature to understand because greater levels of formality imply greater politeness. Indeed, Koreans tend to use formal modes of address (e.g., titles) more often when replying to their recipients by email and are more likely to feel uncomfortable when addressing recipients by their first name. People living in countries with high-context cultures prefer formal communication styles through email (Murphy & Levy, 2006).

East Asians' communication is often viewed as more polite due to the more frequent use of indirect and formal communication styles. When an employee is expected to write an email to a colleague who is a manager vs. one who is a subordinate, communication can change. This is particularly true when in working life, a professional is in a position to request or decline a favor. In those exchanges, politeness strategies are highly associated with communication styles.

To understand how culture impacts forms of politeness, British and South Korean business professionals were described a specific scenario in which they were asked to decline a request for a favor. The professionals were prompted to imagine receiving an email from a junior (or senior) person with whom there was a familiar and positive relationship. In the email, the sender asks the professional for a written character reference letter. However, the professional is very busy due to a large project with tight deadlines and must decline the request (Moon et al., 2019). The professionals were asked to write two versions of the email based on the requester's status (junior vs. senior). They were also asked to record how long it took to write the email and to note which was harder to write and more politely written.

The goal is to understand how much people's communication styles are affected by other people's social status within culture. These samples illustrate the degree to which an interaction partner's status matters for British and Korean people. Of note are differences in communication style that shed light on social hierarchy and politeness.

Cultural Differences in Politeness as a Function of Status Relations

Participants' responses to the prompt illustrated key differences in cultural communication and social values (Moon et al., 2019). An email declining a request made by a senior person compared to a junior person varied greatly between Korean and British communicators. For example, British and Korean professionals differed in how long it took to write the email and how polite they were when declining a senior person's request, but there was no difference between British and Korean professionals in the time taken and politeness invoked when declining a junior person's request.

The emails written by Korean participants (see Box 4.1) were more carefully crafted and evaluated as more polite than those written by British participants (see Box 4.2), which supports a prevalent assumption in literature that East Asians are more polite. However, this assumption may be true only when their interaction partner's status was higher than themselves. British individuals' email communication style and politeness level were very similar, regardless of their interaction partner's hierarchical position, but the hierarchical status of the partner significantly affected Korean individuals' email communication style. Even when the interaction partner is senior, Koreans' email communication style was more polite than the Britons', indicating that Koreans put greater emphasis on relational aspects of hierarchy.

BOX 4.1 KOREAN EMAILS WITH EXPRESSIONS OF APOLOGY

Source: Moon, C., Uskul, A. K., & Weick, M. (2019). Cultural differences in politeness as a function of status relations: Comparing South Korean and British communicators. *Journal of Theoretical Social Psychology,* 3(3), 137–145. https://doi.org/10.1002/jts5.40

Dear senior. Senior, I read the email you sent me. First of all, thank you for giving me the authority to write your recommendation letter. I would like to take a responsibility to write a recommendation letter to meet your expectation, but at this time I have several essays and a team project that I'm in charge of personally. These essays are not only large in volume but also the contents of this team project are detailed and difficult, so I don't think I'll have enough time and ability to write the recommendation letter for you. I'm really sorry. How about talking about the recommendation letter to Gil-Dong? I think he is better than me and he is also your colleague who respects you like me! Thank you and I am sorry.

BOX 4.2 BRITISH EMAILS WITH EXPRESSIONS OF APOLOGY

Source: Moon, C., Uskul, A. K., & Weick, M. (2019). Cultural differences in politeness as afunction of status relations: Comparing South Korean and British communicators. *Journal of Theoretical Social Psychology,* 3(3), 137–145. https://doi.org/10.1002/jts5.40

> Dear Madam,
> I am delighted that you have selected me for a character reference and am very thankful for this. However, as a university student I currently have a heavy work load and am afraid that I will not be able to provide you with the desired reference at this time. I am struggling for time as I am having to work on a group project as well as an extended essay and feel that I should spend my time working on my degree as opposed to writing a reference letter. I hope this does not cause any issues for the need of the letter. Look forward to hearing from you. (name)

Communication styles certainly vary between cultures, but the notion of cultural differences is even more complex than that. East Asians are generally more humble, face-conscious, modest, and indirect communicators (Stadler, 2011), but the East–West cultural differences in politeness levels are most evident in specific socio-hierarchical contexts (e.g., senior vs. junior, boss/manager vs. subordinate) (Moon et al., 2019). In this case, taking into account social status is just as important to understand the cross-cultural differences in communication styles via email as is the desire for harmony.

Use of Apology and Culture

When professionals write an email message to reject a request, they will try to write the content as politely as possible without making the recipient feel unpleasant or uncomfortable. In doing so, they will probably use apologies to highlight the politeness of the message. According to Brown and Levinson (1987), face (i.e., a positive social image that people want to claim for themselves) consists of two basic types: positive (i.e., desire for approval) and negative (i.e., desire for autonomy). The recovery of the recipient's positive or negative face is closely related to the function of apology. In other words, when the communication partner's face is damaged or threatened, apology functions to protect the sender's positive face. Furthermore, apologizing may also be a strategy for managing impressions. An apology may cause the recipient to have a positive image of the sender. Although an apology could be also considered as an act that threatens the face of the message sender because apologizing means admitting wrongdoing, a properly prepared apology which appropriately addresses the type and severity of face-threatening acts can affect the recipient to think more positively about the sender (Holtgraves, 1992; Park et al., 2005).

The concept of apology is universal and exists across cultures. However, people's use and reactions to such apologies may culturally vary. For instance, the preference for direct, elaborate, and extreme forms of apology is higher in Japanese people than in Americans who showed greater preference to explain their behaviors instead of acknowledging them (Barnlund & Yoshioka, 1990; Sugimoto, 1997). This may be because of differently highlighted cultural values: it is important for Japanese people to have harmonious relationships with others under the influence of collectivism, but it is important for Americans to express themselves well and create positive images of themselves under the influence of individualism. In situations where people ask for favors via email, Japanese people tend to use more expressions of apology than gratitude, while Americans tend to use more expressions of gratitude than apology (Lee et al., 2012).

In a similar vein, the use of apology in unsolicited email advertisements was more frequent in Korea compared to the United States where there was almost no expression of apology (Park et al., 2005). Koreans also tended to consider the use of apology as more normal and credible than Americans, and they were more likely to use apology in their own advertising email. The reason why the use of apology is more common and acceptable in East Asian countries may be related to cultural preferences about collectivism and face. Facework strategies of people in collectivistic societies tend to be listener-centered (vs. persuader-centered), putting emphasis on supporting and saving other's social dignity (Ting-Toomey & Kurogi, 1998). In addition, the use of apology would be preferred when the message recipient's social status is higher than the status of the message sender (Moon et al., 2019). The use of apology can be an important tool as a politeness strategy to manage email communication in East Asia.

Use of Gratitude Expression and Culture

While people in East Asian cultures use more expressions of apology to communicate politeness, professionals in Western cultures use gratitude expressions such as "thank you" more commonly. By expressing gratitude in interpersonal communication, the message sender can indicate that the recipient's actions please them. When the gratitude expression is accompanied by a particular form of message that requires the message recipient to pay attention and read the message or accept the request, the gratitude expression may imply some pressure for the message recipient to comply with the goal of the message. That is, the message sender may derive a positive response from the message recipient through the expression of gratitude (Park & Lee, 2012).

The concept of gratitude is also universal and exists across cultures, but the use of gratitude expressions may be culturally varied in relation to situational characteristics and behavioral patterns. For instance, gratitude expressions accepted in one culture may be less accepted in other cultures in which the expression of apology may be used instead. In North America, writing "thank you in advance" is somewhat common in emails asking for favors, while in East Asian cultures like Japan, writing "thank you in advance" may be less common because it could make the sender of the message appear impolite and onerous (Ohashi, 2003). Also, Americans are more likely to use "thank you" in their favor-asking emails compared with Japanese (Lee et al., 2012).

Furthermore, Americans tended to consider the use of gratitude as more positive and credible than Koreans, and they showed higher intention to use expressions of gratitude in their own advertising email (Park & Lee, 2012). This cultural difference could be understood by the relationship between gratitude expressions and face concerns. In the previous section, we found that the expression of apology is a preferred communication strategy among East Asians (Park et al., 2005) since people in collectivistic societies tend to be more concerned about other person's face than those in individualistic societies (Ting-Toomey & Kurogi, 1998). Interestingly, if we consider gratitude expressions as a supportive act for protecting and respecting recipient's positive face, Americans may also be more likely to be concerned about the other person's positive face. In the examples, both Korean (Box 4.3) and British (Box 4.4) participants, even with junior employees, gratitude is clearly expressed.

BOX 4.3 KOREAN EMAILS WITH EXPRESSIONS OF GRATITUDE

Source: Moon, C., Uskul, A. K., & Weick, M. (2019). Cultural differences in politeness as a function of status relations: Comparing South Korean and British communicators. *Journal of Theoretical Social Psychology, 3*(3), 137–145. https://doi.org/10.1002/jts5.40

Thank you for your email. First of all, I would like to thank you for trusting me and asking me for a favor. Unfortunately, however, I am currently in the situation where I can't write the recommendation letter carefully for you, so it will be difficult for me to comply with your request. I think it would be better that you should find someone else as soon as possible. Thank you and I am sorry. If I have a chance, I'd like to help you next time.

> **BOX 4.4 KOREAN EMAILS WITH EXPRESSIONS OF GRATITUDE**
>
> Source: Moon, C., Uskul, A. K., & Weick, M. (2019). Cultural differences in politeness as a function of status relations: Comparing South Korean and British communicators. *Journal of Theoretical Social Psychology, 3*(3), 137–145. https://doi.org/10.1002/jts5.40
>
> Hi there,
>
> Thank you for your email regarding a reference letter. As much as I would like to give you a reference I'm unfortunately very busy at the moment with work and other commitments, and therefore won't have any time to write you a reference letter. Maybe I can suggest emailing another colleague and asking them to write a reference for you? Sorry for the inconvenience caused. Kind Regards

There also may be a cultural difference between the United States and Korea in the use of gratitude expressions; Americans tend to use gratitude expressions (e.g., "thank you") as a phatic expression more often than Koreans do, but Koreans tend to use it when they want to express their true gratitude (Park & Lee, 2012). Thus, the use of gratitude expressions can be considered an important tool as a politeness strategy to manage email communication in Western culture.

Other Factors Affecting Politeness Strategy

Politeness strategy also intersects with relational factors such as power distance and relational distance. People tend to be more polite in their communication styles when the hearer's power is higher than themselves (Ambady et al., 1996; Moon et al., 2019), which is predominantly observed in East Asian countries. In addition to power distance, politeness strategies can be adjusted based on relational distance (Holtgraves, 1992). When you recall your own communication patterns, you may recognize that your style would vary depending on how close or distant your relationship with the interaction partner is (e.g., friend vs. acquaintance/stranger). In your language use, your greatest politeness would be given to those who have higher power and larger distance. Thus, politeness strategies in communication can vary depending on how the relationship between speaker and hearer is defined and established by power distance and relational distance, which too can vary between cultures.

For Koreans, information about age is important in social interaction. Koreans tend to ask about the age of interlocutor to manage the relationship. One of the reasons for this is that interaction in Korean society is based on hierarchy, and hierarchical relationships are confirmed and maintained by language. In particular, the Korean language consists of sophisticated honorifics and the appropriate use of honorific is prescribed by age, status, position, and situation. This rule operates as a social norm. If the rule is violated, interpersonal conflicts may arise. Koreans judge the legitimacy of the use of honorifics based on the age differences between two interlocutors because this is associated with politeness. Koreans widely believe that seniors hold a higher rank than juniors and that they are therefore allowed to speak using informal language to their juniors, whereas juniors must speak using honorifics appropriately by showing their deference to protect the relationships between seniors and juniors. Even if the age gap is only a year, juniors are required to follow the rule. Interestingly, the age effect may not occur in communication with English speakers because of the language difference between English and Korean. The age effect, which indicates the sensitivity of the interaction by the difference in an age, may be culturally specific to Korean society, but in a global organizational context, it is necessary to understand the effect of age along with other cultural values when it comes to successfully managing intercultural communication.

Conclusion

The concept of politeness exists across cultures, and, undeniably, being polite is important in interpersonal professional communication. According to Brown and Levinson's (1987) politeness theory, the strategic use of polite expressions based on a universal concern to save or support face of oneself and others may be the key to successful management of interpersonal communication. However, cultural differences in communication styles must be considered. For instance, individuals in East Asian cultures tend to use more high-context communication styles (e.g., indirect) that are based on relational concerns and politeness principles, while people in Western cultures tend to use more low-context communication styles (e.g., direct) that entail being more open and precise. Hence, we may agree with a prevalent assumption that East Asians are generally indirect, face-conscious, and modest communicators, and their communication style is more polite than people living in other cultural groups. However, the assumption may not always be true since the East–West cultural differences in politeness level and strategies can be moderated by relationship status between communicators.

Moreover, cultural differences also exist in the expression of politeness. While members of East Asian societies tend to use more apology expressions, members of Western societies tend to use more gratitude expressions. Since communication styles and politeness strategies vary from culture to culture, it is important to enhance our understanding of cultural influences on communication to achieve successful intercultural communication in a globalized world.

Discussion Questions

- Was the email communication style of British or Koreans more polite and for what reasons?
- What are the two basic types of face as defined by Brown and Levinson (1987)?
- Why is the use of an apology more common and acceptable in East Asian countries?
- In which context are gratitude expressions more accepted and why?
- Which politeness strategies do East Asian people and Western cultures, respectively, tend to use?
- How do considerations of age factor into politeness strategies and in which context(s)?

Suggestions for Further Reading

Hofstede, G. H., Hofstede, G. J., & Minkov, M. (2010). *Cultures and organizations: Software for the mind.* New York: McGraw-Hill.

Moon, C., Uskul, A. K., & Weick, M. (2019). Cultural differences in politeness as a function of status relations: Comparing South Korean and British communicators. *Journal of Theoretical Social Psychology, 3*(3), 137–145. https://doi.org/10.1002/jts5.40

Stadler, S. (2011). Intercultural communication and East Asian politeness. In D. Kádár & S. Mills (Eds.), *Politeness in East Asia* (pp. 98–124). Cambridge, UK: Cambridge University Press.

References

Ambady, N., Koo, J., Lee, F., & Rosenthal, R. (1996). More than words: Linguistic and nonlinguistic politeness in two cultures. *Journal of Personality and Social Psychology, 70,* 996–1011. https://doi.org/10.1037/0022-3514.70.5.996

Ayers, E. (1984). Vengeance and justice. New York: Oxford.

Barnlund, D. C., & Yoshioka, M. (1990). Apologies: Japanese and American styles. *International Journal of Intercultural Relations, 14*(2), 193–206. https://doi.org/10.1016/0147-1767(90)90005-H

Brown, P., & Levinson, S. C. (1987). *Politeness: Some universals in language usage.* Cambridge, MA: Cambridge University Press.

Goffman, E. (1967). *Interaction ritual.* Garden City, NY: Anchor Books.

Goldsmith, D. J., & Lamb Normand, E. (2015). Politeness theory: How we use language to save face. In D. O. Braithwaite & P. Schrodt (Eds.), *Engaging theories in interpersonal communication: Multiple perspectives* (2nd ed., pp. 267–278). Thousand Oaks, CA: Sage.

Gudykunst, W. B. (2001). *Asian American ethnicity and communication.* Thousand Oaks, CA: Sage.
Hall, E. T. (1976). *Beyond culture.* Garden City, NY: Anchor Press/Double Day.
Ho, D.Y. (1976). On the concept of face. *American Journal of Sociology,* 81(4), 867–884. https://doi.org/10.1086/226145
Holtgraves, T. (1992). The linguistic realization of face management: Implications for language production and comprehension, person perception, and cross-cultural communication. *Social Psychology Quarterly,* 55(2), 141–159. https://doi.org/10.2307/2786943
Lee, H. E., Park, H. S., Imai, T., & Dolan, D. (2012). Cultural differences between Japan and the United States in uses of "apology" and "thank you" in favor asking messages. *Journal of Language and Social Psychology,* 31(3), 263–289. https://doi.org/10.1177/0261927X12446595
Moon, C., Uskul, A. K., & Weick, M. (2019). Cultural differences in politeness as a function of status relations: Comparing South Korean and British communicators. *Journal of Theoretical Social Psychology,* 3(3), 137–145. https://doi.org/10.1002/jts5.40
Murphy, M., & Levy, M. (2006). Politeness in intercultural email communication: Australian and Korean perspectives. *Journal of Intercultural Communication, 12,* 1–12.
Norton, R. (1983). *Communicator style.* Beverly Hills, CA: Sage.
Ohashi, J. (2003). Japanese culture specific face and politeness orientation: A pragmatic investigation of yoroshiku onegaishimasu. *Multilingua,* 22(3), 257–274. https://doi.org/10.1515/mult.2003.013
Park, H. S., & Lee, H. E. (2012). Cultural differences in "thank you". *Journal of Language and Social Psychology,* 31(2), 138–156. https://doi.org/10.1177/0261927X12438536
Park, H. S., Lee, H. E., & Song, J. A. (2005). "I am sorry to send you SPAM" cross-cultural differences in use of apologies in email advertising in Korea and the US. *Human Communication Research,* 31(3), 365–398. https://doi.org/10.1111/j.1468-2958.2005.tb00876.x
Searle, J. (1969). *Speech acts: An essay in the philosophy of language.* Cambridge, UK: Cambridge University.
Sugimoto, N. (1997). A Japan–U.S. comparison of apology styles. *Communication Research,* 24(4), 349–369. https://doi.org/10.1177%2F009365097024004002
Ting-Toomey, S., & Kurogi, A. (1998). Facework competence in intercultural conflict: An updated face-negotiation theory. *International Journal of Intercultural Relations,* 22(2), 187–225. https://doi.org/10.1016/S0147-1767(98)00004-2
Zhong, C.-B., Magee, J., Maddux, W., & Galinsky, A. D. (2006). Power, culture, and (in)action: Considerations in the expression and enactment of power in East Asian and Western society. In B. Mannix, M. Neale, & Y. Chen (Eds.), *Research on managing groups and teams: National culture & groups* (Vol. 9, pp. 53–73). Oxford, UK: Elsevier Science Press.

PART 2
Group and Organizational Contexts

5
PERCEPTIONS OF COWORKER TRUSTWORTHINESS IN JAPAN AND THE UNITED STATES

Masami Nishishiba

Trust is a widely used concept in everyday life. Sociologist Bernard Barber (1983) aptly observed "nearly everyone seems to be talking about 'trust.' Presidential candidates, political columnists, pollsters, social critics, moral philosophers, and the man in the street, all use the word freely and earnestly" (p. 1). Trust is a key concept in business communication, where building trust is frequently highlighted as an important factor in interpersonal and intercultural relations (e.g., Langlinais, Howard, & Houghton, 2022). Trust is also recognized to improve group efficiency (e.g., Cheng et al., 2021). This chapter highlights how individualistic and collectivist cultural differences influence perceptions of trustworthy coworkers in Japan and the United States.

Conceptualization of Trust and Trustworthiness

Despite its widely claimed importance, trust is an intangible concept. There is no consensus on the conceptualization of trust (Kee & Knox, 1970; Pearce, 1974). Some scholars define trust as confidence toward others for a set of expectations, some study trust as a personality trait, and some examine trust in relation to risk assessment (Bachmann & Zaheer, 2006).

In organizational contexts, trust has been identified as a critical aspect for high organizational performance (Dirks & Ferrin, 2001). Trust is positively associated with a number of performance indicators, such as productivity, job satisfaction, problem-solving effectiveness, and information flow.

Studies in the United States have identified a number of key factors needed for business persons to gain trust from their coworkers including:

DOI: 10.4324/9781003298199-8

- *Accessibility/receptivity* means being open and receptive to giving and accepting ideas. For example, an accessible executive is "one who takes in ideas easily and gives them out freely" (Jennings, 1971, p. 148), and who does not ridicule other people's ideas.
- *Availability* is defined as being physically present when needed. A trusted executive is the one who "learns to be available at certain times in case his superior sends down for information or suggestions" (Jennings, 1971, p. 149).
- *Competence* refers to knowledge and skills related to a specific task, to the ability to get the job done, and to make right decisions (Butler, 1991; Mishra, 1996).
- *Concern* addresses how one takes interest in the "welfare of the entire organization" (Mishra, 1996, p. 267) as well as the people they work with.
- *Discreteness* refers to not sharing sensitive or confidential information with others (Butler, 1991).
- *Fairness* is the characteristic of treating people on an equal basis with others in the same circumstances (Butler, 1991).
- *Integrity* refers to being honest and not telling lies and, in a business context, fulfilling commitments (Butler, 1991).
- *Openness* describes how people willingly give and share ideas and information (Butler, 1991). It is associated with honesty; it emphasizes the importance of telling subordinates the truth without concealment (Mishra, 1996).
- *Loyalty* is an implicit promise from persons that they will not bring harm to the other. For example, an executive will lose trust for a subordinate who exposes a superior's errors for personal gain (Jennings, 1971).
- *Predictability or consistency* (Butler, 1991; Jennings, 1971) means acting and making decisions in a consistent fashion. When a superior knows a subordinate, or a machine for that matter, will always make decisions according to standards, trust is improved by predictability (Jennings, 1971).
- *Promise fulfillment* refers to how well a person follows through on promises; it is an essential component in integrity (Butler, 1991).
- *Reliability/dependability* refers to a consistent coordination between a person's words, promises, and actions (Mishra, 1996).

Clearly, trust is a multidimensional concept that encompasses a number of factors, but in different cultural contexts, individuals may interpret them very differently.

Cultural Dimensions: Individualism vs. Collectivism

Communication behaviors are linked to both cultural and psychological dimensions, which means that they are simultaneously related to people and things in society and to the individual's personality. As Singelis put it, "culture affects the development of an individual's psychological makeup, which in turn, affects communication behavior" (Singelis & Brown, 1995, p. 355). Culture is not merely an influence from something that remains outside a person. It is also internalized into the cognitive structures and processes of the individual, and expressed independently (Bruner, 1990; D'Andrade, 1990).

Individualism/collectivism is a dimension of culture that has been related to differences in individual behavior. The distinction has been broadly applied, and a body of studies shows that a scale of individualism/collectivism can be useful to distinguish cultural differences in individuals and their group relationships (Hofstede, Hofstede, & Minkov, 2010; Triandis, 1995).

Individualism is a cultural preference to be independent from any social group. In an individualist culture, people are motivated primarily by their own preferences, needs, and rights. An individualist sense gives priority to personal goals over collective goals. In an individualist culture, a person's self-image is defined in terms of "I" as an independent self (Markus & Kitayama, 1991). This attitude emphasizes autonomy, emotional independence, personal initiative, right to privacy, pleasure seeking, financial security, selective friendships, and universal rules. People in an individualist culture tend to have less attachment to the groups they belong to; they "pick and choose so as to maximize their 'profit' and minimize the 'cost' of membership" (Triandis, 1989, p. 61).

Collectivism is a cultural preference to identify with one or more social groups. In a collectivist culture, people are motivated primarily by the standards of social groups they belong to. A collectivist sense gives priority to the ways of a group over the individual (Nishishiba, 2018, p. 18). In a collectivist culture, a person's self-image is defined in terms of "we" as an interdependent self enmeshed in group relationships (Markus & Kitayama, 1991). This attitude emphasizes collective identity, emotional dependence, group solidarity, sharing, duties and obligations, stable and predetermined friendships, group decisions, and particular rules for specific roles in the group. People in a collectivist culture are emotionally attached to a few groups and tend to be very concerned about preserving and promoting these groups (Triandis, 1989).

Cultural Contexts: Japan and the United States

This case study highlights the cultural differences in businesspeople's perceptions of trustworthy coworkers between Japan and the United States.

Japan is known to have a culture with a collectivist orientation. One indication of collectivism is seen in the social importance of having an in-group and group belongingness in Japanese society (e.g., Zander, 1983).

The Japanese commonly distinguish those in an in-group (*uchi*, meaning "inside") versus an out-group (*soto*, meaning "outside") that is less valued. There is a strong desire to accomplish *ittaikan* ("feeling oneness") with those in the in-group (Lebra, 1976). In business contexts in Japan, importance is placed on the goals and needs of the company, and harmonious relationships with people in the company, over those who pursue individual goals.

The United States is known to have a culture with an individualist orientation. In the United States, "individual personality rather than group identity and responsibility" is valued, and "the individual [is] an integral agent, relatively autonomous and morally responsible" (Williams, 1970, p. 482). In U.S. business contexts, making a right individual decision even at the risk of creating conflicts with others tends to be more valued.

Conceptualizatons of Trust in Japan and the United States

This section discusses some differences in the concept of trustworthiness between Japanese and U.S. businesspeople, focusing on two main areas of interest. The category of organizational commitment is emphasized by Japanese businesspeople, and the category of personal integrity is emphasized by U.S. businesspeople. Cultural orientations toward collectivism by the Japanese and individualism by the Americans can help to explain the differences.

Cultural Differences in Terms Associated with Trust

To understand possible differences in the conceptualization of trustworthiness among these two cultures, business people from Japan and the United States were asked to sort a set of 30 cards that contained words associated with trustworthiness (see Table 5.1).

TABLE 5.1 Terms linked to trustworthiness

Availability	*Receptivity*	*Conscientiousness*
Personal integrity	Consistency	Have common sense
Organized	Committed	Competence
Considerate	Cooperative	Dependable/reliable
Being discreet	Do job in a timely manner	Do what they say they do
experienced	Fairness	Have positive attitude
Honest	Knowledgeable	Loyalty
Not sneaky	Openness	Fulfill promises
Worthy of respect	Responsible	Sincere
Supportive	Truthful	Try to do a better job

Each participant sorted the 30 cards into groupings based on perceived similarities of the words. Once the sorting was complete, participants were then asked to look at each group and think of a single word or phrase that best described it. Japanese businesspeople divided the words into five groups: (1) responsible behavior, (2) professional competence, (3) organizational commitment, (4) relational quality, and (5) communication (see Table 5.2). U.S. businesspeople divided the words on trustworthiness into four groups: (1) responsible behavior, (2) professional competence, (3) relational quality, and (4) personal integrity (see Table 5.3). These groupings correspond with two higher-level categories: organizational and personal qualities of trustworthiness.

Groupings of words related to trustworthiness by Japanese and U.S. businesspeople highlighted some similarities as well as differences in the way they understand the concept. Both groups clearly distinguished organizational and personal qualities, and agreed on general organizational characteristics of responsible behavior and professional competence, and a personal relational quality. Notable differences between the two groups included additional categories for Japanese businesspeople emphasizing organizational commitment and personal communication qualities, and for U.S. businesspeople, an additional emphasis on personal integrity.

Organizational Commitment

Japanese businesspeople gave special attention to organizational commitment as an attribute of trustworthiness. Organizational commitment is "an employee's belief in and acceptance of his or her organization's goals and values, willingness to exert effort on that organization's behalf, and desire to remain employed there" (Allen & Brady, 1997, p. 320). These attributes of commitment are more important to Japanese businesspeople than to U.S. businesspeople as indicators of trustworthiness.

This emphasis on organizational commitment is consistent with previous research on Japanese management. For example, "In the contemporary Japanese organization, allegiance to the corporation is of utmost importance. Individual careers are subsumed by the commitment to a single company. Particularly within the larger Japanese corporation, a fierce, lifelong loyalty tends to prevail" (Goldman, 1994, p. 99). Sullivan notes that the Japanese notion of "work" differs from the United States and explains that for the Japanese "work is simply living as one is supposed to live in accord with the order of society. It is a process of carrying out obligations owed to society and to oneself as a social being" (1992, p. 90).

This notion of work as a process of living may have deep religious roots. Shozan Suzuki, a seventeenth-century Zen Buddhist, stated, "If you cast aside all attachments and work hard, the gods will favor you, and your

TABLE 5.2 Trustworthiness groupings by Japanese businesspeople

Higher-Level Grouping	Organizational Qualities			Personal Qualities	
Grouping Name	Responsible Behavior	Professional Competence	Organizational Commitment	Relational Quality	Communication
Words	• Fulfill promises • Responsible • Consistency • Do what they say they do • Do job in a timely manner • Being discreet • Integrity	• Experienced • Knowledgeable • Competence • Organized • Have common sense • Worthy of respect	• Committed • Try to do a better job • Loyalty • Have positive attitude	• Availability • Supportive • Considerate • Receptivity • Dependable/reliable • Cooperative	• Honest • Truthful • Sincere • Not sneaky • Fairness • Openness • Conscientious

TABLE 5.3 Trustworthiness groupings by U.S. businesspeople

Higher-Level Grouping	Organizational Qualities		Personal Qualities	
Grouping Name	Responsible Behavior	Professional Competence	Relational Quality	Personal Integrity
Words	• Fulfill promises • Responsible • Consistency • Do what they say they do • Dependable/reliable • Committed • Conscientious • Try to do a better job • Have common sense	• Experienced • Knowledgeable • Competence • Organized • Do job in a timely manner	• Availability • Supportive • Considerate • Receptivity • Have a positive attitude • Openness • Cooperative	• Honest • Truthful • Sincere • Not sneaky • Fairness • Loyalty • Being discreet • Worthy of respect • Integrity

profits will be considerable. You will become a person of virtue and wealth, but you will care nothing for that wealth" (cited in Seward & Van Zandt, 1985). This kind of idea propagated in traditional Zen Buddhism might have influenced ideas about work as moral as well as instrumental. Commitment to work is associated with being a good human being.

In this light, it makes sense that a Japanese businessperson would tend to judge trustworthiness based on commitment to the organization. The work relationship is an act of allegiance and an expression of loyalty (Sullivan, 1992). Work is what one does as a respected member of the community, regardless of what one gets out of it personally.

Sullivan (1992) also contrasted organizational commitment among Japanese and U.S. workers, who view work mainly as an economic transaction. U.S. workers tend to be motivated by promised compensation in an exchange relationship. Hard work and a hard-work ethic are encouraged in the United States as in the Protestant work ethic, yet in current conditions, the principle of exchange remains central to the work relationship. For example, studies of U.S. employees (Allen & Brady, 1997; Johnson, 1993) found organizational commitment increased when employees perceived that their increased efforts to reach organizational goals were noticed and rewarded by the organization. Consequently, recommendations to improve organizational commitment among U.S. workers focus on reciprocal relationships and mutual exchange between employees and their organization.

Personal Integrity

Emphasis on personal integrity by U.S. businesspeople emerged as another difference in the understanding of trustworthiness. The importance of personal integrity as a key aspect of trustworthiness in U.S. contexts has been observed by other researchers. For example, in worker interviews about trust, integrity was emphasized as an important character trait as individuals "felt that, without a perception of the other's 'moral character' and 'basic honesty,' other dimensions of trust were meaningless" (Butler & Cantell, 1984, p. 20). In another study, 93.5% of the respondents viewed trust as "a belief in the integrity, character, and ability of others" (Mishra & Morrissey, 1990, p. 443).

Shaw (1997) developed a model of trust with three basic conditions: achieve results, act with integrity, and demonstrate concern. Integrity is adherence to a code of ethics or set of values and involves how well our actions match our beliefs. It suggests a wholeness or coherence in our philosophies and values, in our public and private statements, and in our actions across a variety of situations. Integrity is thus a measure of coherence and consistency, and it is key to building and sustaining trust. In sum, we trust those who are honest in what they say and consistent in how they act (p. 61).

However, the notion of personal integrity did not emerge as a key aspect in the Japanese concept of trustworthiness. Examining how the word "integrity" appeared in the word groupings by Japanese businesspeople gives an interesting insight on how the Japanese conceive integrity in relation to trustworthiness. In the Japanese groupings, the word "integrity" appeared as an organizational quality under the label "responsible behavior," grouped with words such as "do what they say they do," "consistency," "fulfill promises," "responsible," "being discreet," and "do job in a timely manner." Here, integrity is associated with coherence and consistency in organizational—not individual—behavior. This difference from U.S. businesspeople who grouped integrity as a distinct personal quality may have meaningful consequences in business interactions.

Trustworthiness: Interdependent and Independent Views

This study suggests that the concept of trustworthiness by Japanese businesspeople is influenced by a collectivist orientation, while the concept of trustworthiness by U.S. businesspeople is influenced by an individualist orientation. Japanese businesspeople tended to judge trustworthiness of coworkers by how the individual relates to the group and the organization, while U.S. businesspeople judged trustworthiness of coworkers by personal qualities that fit in any situation, regardless of the group or organizational affiliation.

The Japanese concept of trustworthiness can be described as an "interdependent view," whereas the U.S. concept is an "independent view." A collectivist orientation associates individuals as part of a group, and personal attributes are judged by how an individual acts as a member of a group; hence, the view of trustworthiness becomes more interdependent.

In contrast, an individualist orientation tends to see an autonomous individual, judged by individual merits (Triandis, 1995). An individualist, independent orientation tends to view an individual character in abstract, context-free qualities (Markus & Kitayama, 1991; Shweder & Bourne, 1982). Further, an individual is "viewed as an autonomous entity endowed with independent rights and desires who relates to others in terms of self-interest and negotiated agreements" (Schwartz, 1994, p. 95).

A collectivist orientation tends to overlap personal goals with the goals of an in-group and considers it obvious that one ought to subordinate personal goals to group goals (Triandis, 1995). A judgment of trustworthiness in a person's character is not independent in the person but interdependent with that person's actions in the group.

Implications for Practitioners

Assumptions about trustworthiness may differ according to a person's social origin in a collectivist or individualist culture. These differences can lead to misevaluations of each other. This chapter highlights the importance of checking one's own and others' assumptions when communicating and working with people from a different culture.

In terms of trustworthiness, this research suggests that a Japanese worker may perceive a U.S. colleague who does not subordinate personal goals to the organization's goals to be untrustworthy due to inadequate organizational commitment. A U.S. coworker may see no issue with the same colleague and may even take an opposite view, perceiving a colleague to be too much like a "yes" person who does whatever the boss asks, and hence untrustworthy as an individual.

Recognizing these cultural differences in the concept of trustworthiness can help prevent misunderstandings and negative judgments. Communicating openly about underlying assumptions in a multicultural organization might be useful, giving employees a space and language to take account of each other, and better interpret their own and others' messages and actions. For those who intend to engage in a multinational/multicultural team, mutual trust may be enhanced by advanced multicultural training.

Conclusion

The study described in this chapter identified important differences between Japanese and U.S. concepts of trustworthiness in business. In a test sorting 30 trust-related words, Japanese businesspeople tended to give greater emphasis to organizational commitment as a sign of trustworthiness, and U.S. businesspeople tended to give greater emphasis to personal integrity as an autonomous individual. These differences correspond to cultural orientations on a collectivism/individualism scale and interdependent/independent views of trustworthiness.

The differences between a Japanese collectivist culture and a U.S. individualist culture are well known. Global professionals benefit when they hold the awareness of specific differences in judgments of trustworthiness in the forefront of their business interactions. Better understanding of such key concepts among intercultural partners may help improve personal communication as well as organizational well-being.

Discussion Questions

- Think about someone you think is trustworthy. What makes this person trustworthy?

- Try it yourself. Sort the 30 words by similarities. How are your groupings similar and different from the Japanese and U.S. businesspeople? How might your own cultural orientation explain those similarities and differences?
- What might explain the unique groupings by Japanese businesspeople related to organizational commitment and communication?
- What might explain the unique grouping by U.S. businesspeople related to personal integrity?
- How might these differences relate to differences in cultural orientation toward collectivism and individualism?
- How do you think different concepts of trustworthiness might affect interactions between Japanese and U.S. businesspeople in specific organizational situations (e.g., negotiations, hiring, change management)?

Suggestions for Further Reading

Buttigieg, P. (2020). *Trust: America's best chance*. New York: Liveright.

Covey, S. M. R., Link, G., & Merrill, R. R. (2012). *Smart trust: Creating prosperity, energy, and joy in a low-trust world*. New York: Free Press.

Gudykunst, W. B., Matsumoto, Y., Ting-Toomey, S., Nishida, T., Kim, K., & Heyman, S. (1996). The influence of cultural individualism-collectivism, self construals, and individual values on communication styles across cultures. *Human Communication Research, 22*(4), 510–543.

Kee, H. W., & Knox, R. E. (1970). Conceptual and methodological considerations in the study of trust and suspicion. *The Journal of Conflict Resolution, 14*(3), 357–366.

Kouzes, J. M., & Posner, B. Z. (2011). *Credibility: How leaders gain and lose it, why people demand it* (2nd ed.). Hoboken, NJ: John Wiley & Sons.

Kramer, R. M., & Tyler, T. R. (1996). *Trust in organizations*. Thousand Oaks, CA: Sage.

References

Allen, M. W., & Brady, R. M. (1997). Total quality management, organizational commitment, perceived organizational support, and intraorganizational communication. *Management Communication Quarterly, 10*(3), 316–341.

Bachmann, R., & Zaheer, A. (2006). *Handbook of trust research*. Cheltenham: Edward Elgar Publishing.

Barber, B. (1983). *The logic and limits of political trust*. New York: New Brunswick.

Bruner, J. (1990). *Acts of meaning*. Cambridge, MA: Harvard University Press.

Butler, J. K., Jr. (1991). Toward understanding and measuring conditions of trust: Evolution of a conditions of trust inventory. *Journal of Management, 17*(3), 643–663.

Butler, J. K., Jr., & Cantrell, R. S. (1984). A behavioral decision theory approach to modeling dyadic trust in superiors and subordinates. *Psychological Reports, 55*(1), 19–28.

Cheng, X., Bao, Y., Yu, X., & Shen, Y. (2021). Trust and group efficiency in multinational virtual team collaboration: A longitudinal study. *Group Decision and Negotiation, 30*(3), 529–551.

D'Andrade, R. (1990). Some propositions about the relations between culture and human cognition. In J. W. Stigler, R. A. Shweder & G. Herdt (Eds.), Cultural psychology: Essays on comparative human development (pp. 65–129). Cambridge: Cambridge University Press. https://doi.org/10.1017/CBO9781139173728.004

Dirks, K. T., & Ferrin, D. L. (2001). The role of trust in organizational settings. *Organization Science, 12*(4), 450–467. https://doi.org/10.1287/orsc.12.4.450.10640

Goldman, A. (1994). *Doing business with the Japanese: A guide to successful communication, management, and diplomacy.* Albany, NY: Suny Press.

Hofstede, G. H., Hofstede, G. J., & Minkov, M. (2010). *Cultures and organizations: Software of the mind* (3rd ed.). Maidenhead: McGraw-Hill.

Jennings, E. E. (1971). *Routes to the executive suite.* New York: McGraw-Hill.

Johnson, R. S. (1993). *TQM: Management processes for quality operations.* Milwaukee, WI: ASQC Quality Press.

Kee, H. W., & Knox, R. E. (1970). Conceptual and methodological considerations in the study of trust and suspicion. *Journal of Conflict Resolution, 14*(3), 357–366.

Langlinais, L. A., Howard, H. A., & Houghton, J. D. (2022). Trust me: Interpersonal communication dominance as a tool for influencing interpersonal trust between coworkers. *International Journal of Business Communication.* https//doi.org/10.1177/23294884221080933

Lebra, T. S. (1976). *Japanese patterns of behavior.* Honolulu: University of Hawaii Press.

Markus, H. R., & Kitayama, S. (1991). Culture and the self: Implications for cognition, emotion, and motivation. *Psychological Review, 98*(2), 224–253.

Mishra, A. K. (1996). Organizational responses to crisis. In *Trust in organizations: Frontiers of theory and research* (pp. 261–287). Thousand Oaks, CA: Sage.

Mishra, J., & Morrissey, M. A. (1990). Trust in employee/employer relationships: A survey of West Michigan managers. *Public Personnel Management, 19*(4), 443–486.

Nishishiba, M. (2018). *Culturally mindful communication: Essential skills for public and nonprofit professionals.* Milton Park: Routledge.

Pearce, W. B. (1974). Trust in interpersonal communication. *Communication Monographs, 41,* 236–244.

Schwartz, S. H. (1994). Beyond individualism/collectivism: New cultural dimensions of values. In U. Kim, H. C. Triandis, Ç. Kâğitçibaşi, S. C. Choi, & G. Yoon (Eds.), *Individualism and collectivism: Theory, method, and applications* (pp. 85–119). Thousand Oaks, CA: Sage.

Seward, J., & Van Zandt, H. F. (1985). *Japan, the hungry guest: Japanese business ethics vs. those of the US.* Tokyo: Yohan.

Shaw, R. B. (1997). *Trust in the balance: Building successful organizations on results, integrity, and concern.* San Francisco, CA: Jossey-Bass.

Shweder, R. A., & Bourne, E. J. (1982). Does the concept of the person vary cross-culturally? In A. Marsella & G. White (Eds.), *Cultural conceptions of mental health and therapy* (pp. 97–137). Dordrecht: Springer Science + Business Media.

Singelis, T. M., & Brown, W. J. (1995). Culture, self, and collectivist communication: Linking culture to individual behavior. *Human Communication Research, 21*(3), 354–389.

Sullivan, J. J. (1992). *Invasion of the salarymen*: Westport, CT: Praeger Publishers.

Triandis, H. C. (1989). The self and social behavior in differing cultural contexts. *Psychological Review, 96*(3), 506–520. https://doi.org/10.1037/0033-295X.96.3.506

Triandis, H. C. (1995). *Individualism & collectivism*. Boulder, CO: Westview Press.

Williams, R. M. (1970). *American society: A sociological interpretation*. New York: Knopf.

Zander, A. (1983). The value of belonging to a group in Japan. *Small Group Behavior, 14*(1), 3–14.

6
CULTURAL DIMENSIONS OF ORGANIZATIONAL LOYALTY IN GERMANY AND CHINA

Stephan Meschke and Juana Du

Employee loyalty is commonly referred to as if it were a switch—an employee is either loyal or not. But this understanding is limited. Levels of employee loyalty exist on a continuum, ranging from disloyal to non-loyal at the negative end to loyal and hyper-loyal at the positive end. Employee loyalty is active, deliberate, voluntary, and reciprocal behavior that is characterized by different reference objects and levels. These different levels have a significant influence on the outcomes of a company.

The theory of psychological contract helps to explain employee loyalty. The psychological contract is an implicit and informal complement to the written and formal employment contract (Thompson & Bunderson, 2003). Similar to employee loyalty, the psychological contract is mostly hidden in employees' minds and is strongly subject to individual perceptions. Moreover, it is based on reciprocity (Coyle-Shapiro & Kessler, 2002). This means that employees and companies define reciprocal expectations of each other and are each clear about the commitment and returns that should flow from this relationship (De Vos, Buyens, & Schalk, 2003). Furthermore, the psychological contract is considered dynamic and changing over the working period (Herriot & Pemberton, 1997). As with employee loyalty, the positive buildup takes a relatively long time, whereas unfulfilled promises and breaches of the psychological contract can have a very rapid and immediately negative effect.

Cultural Dimensions of Loyalty

In the organizational context, loyalty is characterized by reference objects: supervisor, working group, and organization. The weight of reference

DOI: 10.4324/9781003298199-9

objects always depends on cultural background. Various studies examine employee loyalty in the context of different national cultures. For simplicity, employee loyalty can be categorized in terms of "Western" cultures in contrast with those in "Eastern" cultures. Western cultures tend to be characterized rather by low power distance and high individualism. Eastern cultures, on the other hand, often express strong power distance and high collectivism (Hofstede, 2015). In addition, cultural standards such as social harmony, group orientation, face approach, or hierarchy orientation have a high importance especially in the Chinese context, which should be considered in the concept of employee loyalty.

Employee loyalty in Germany as a Western culture can be defined by three reference objects, while in China as an Eastern culture there are only two reference objects (see Meschke, 2021). The reference objects such as supervisor, working group, and organization were identified in a German survey as the areas where employees placed loyalty, which is why we can speak of "Tripartite Employee Loyalty" (TEL). This means that companies must take these three sub-loyalties into account when considering the loyalty of their employees, as they do not all have to be equally strong but can work in different directions. For example, if the employees in a work group show a higher level of loyalty to the company compared to the average loyalty level across the three, this is initially good news from the company's point of view. However, if the employee's loyalty to the supervisor is even higher, this can lead to an exodus of employees if the supervisor leaves. Therefore, in the German/Western cultural area, it is important to balance a healthy degree of loyalty across these three reference objects.

The same investigation of Chinese workers found that that employee loyalty was directed at working group and organization/supervisor. The reason for this seems to be the cultural peculiarity that the manager is not only perceived as a representative of a company, but rather embodies a company directly. Thus, a "Bipartite Employee Loyalty" (BEL) approach is more likely to emerge in Eastern cultures.

Effects of Employee Loyalty

Expectations for employee loyalty have evolved over time and can no longer be understood as tacit agreement, lifelong company affiliation, or one-dimensional dependencies (Meschke, 2021). Even though employee loyalty is as strong as it has been historically, it is still the focus of many practical publications and academic discussions because of its impact on positive and negative behaviors.

Employee loyalty has a number of positive effects on employee behavior. Loyal employees are better at resolving conflicts (Luchak, 2003), have less intention to leave the employer (Chen, 2001), produce higher service quality (Yee, Yeung, & Cheng, 2010), and exert extra effort for the company (James & Cropanzano, 1994). Loyalty can also offset negative behaviors. For example, employees who resist changes are likely to be more flexible if they feel more loyalty.

Work overload, on the other hand, is a more difficult behavioral pattern that does not seem to decrease or increase proportionally with the loyalty level. In general, it can be said that complete sacrifice for an employer can result in conflicts with family, stress, and burnout (Tabarsa et al., 2013). Overcommitment clouds the perception of effort and reward and therefore has a negative impact on employee health (Siegrist et al., 2004). Especially hyper-loyal employees are at risk of work overload, as self-loyalty can be set aside to the advantage of employee loyalty.

Cultural Contexts: Germany and China

The comparison of German and Chinese cultural standards provides an indication of possible differences in national employee loyalty. Germany is known to be fact- and rule-oriented. Communication is very direct, and the important parts of the conversation are conveyed through words. In addition, emphasis is placed on time management and punctuality as well as the separation of personality and areas of life. In China, on the other hand, social harmony is the highest principle of interpersonal relationships. Therefore, rules are always interpreted relatively and mistakes are not directly addressed. In addition, much time is invested in maintaining personal networks, the *quanxi*, which are in a strict hierarchical order.

Employee Conceptualizations of Loyalty

German and Chinese employees from two large health-care organizations in Germany and China responded to surveys about how they perceived and performed loyalty. Though Germany and China represent two very different national cultures, both companies stem from parent companies with over 10,000 employees. Additionally, all of the employees who were surveyed belonged to the service-oriented sectors of their respective companies. The results of the surveys demonstrate that German and Chinese employees conceptualize loyalty very differently.

German Conceptualizations of Loyalty

Employees in the service sector of a large German health-care organization clearly acknowledged each of the reference objects: loyalty to organization, loyalty to working group, and loyalty to supervisor, and each of the reference objects was clarified further by three distinct factors (see Table 6.1). German employees reflected greater organizational loyalty by wearing the company logo and promoting their company's reputation externally to friends and internally against disparagement. Loyalty to their working teams was performed by engaging in the team, taking on extra group work (to benefit the team members), and speaking against criticism of their working team members or team efforts. The third reference object, loyalty to supervisor, was performed by agreeing with the supervisor's opinions, defending

TABLE 6.1 Employee loyalty concept (Exploratory Factor Analysis, German sample)

Items	Factors		
	A. Loyalty to Organization	B. Loyalty to Working Group	C. Loyalty to Supervisor
A Loyalty to Organization			
1 Also in my spare time I wear clothing (caps, jackets, lanyards, etc.) that bears the company's symbol or insignia (or I would do so if my company had such clothing).	0.88		
2 I speak highly of the company to friends.	0.66		
3 I defend my organization when other employees criticize it.	0.63		
B Loyalty to Working Group			
1 I take an active part in my working group's affairs.		0.82	
2 I do more than one's share of the working group task.		0.79	
3 I defend the honor of my working group whenever it is unfairly criticized.		0.64	
C Loyalty to Supervisor			
1 I agree with my supervisor's opinions.			0.89
2 When somebody speaks ill of my supervisor, I will defend him/her immediately.			0.85
3 I tell my colleagues or friends about my supervisor's merits.			0.81
Cronbach's alpha	0.65	0.68	0.84

Note
Loadings > 0.4 are reported, $N = 148$.

TABLE 6.2 Employee loyalty concept with negative outcomes (correlations, German sample)

Variable	Mean	Standard Deviation	1	2	3	4
1 Loyalty to Organization	5.66	0.93				
2 Loyalty to Working Group	6.01	1.00	0.47**			
3 Loyalty to Supervisor	4.73	1.29	0.33**	0.27**		
4 TEL	5.46	0.87	0.65**	0.60**	0.64**	
5 Work Overload	3.69	1.32	0.04	0.01	−0.07	−0.01

Note
Kendall rank correlation method was applied, $N = 148$.
*Correlations are statistically significant at $p < 0.05$; **correlations are statistically significant at $p < 0.01$.

the supervisor against disparaging remarks, and promoting the supervisor to individuals both internally and externally. Much of German employee loyalty is performed by promoting or defending the organization, working groups, or the supervisors.

Further, German employees from this sample perceived and performed loyalty across the three reference objects. As Table 6.2 shows, the factors all correlate significantly with each other and with the overall TEL scale. One unique finding was that, for work overload, there is no correlation. Despite the expectation that increased loyalty leads to an increased commitment to working more, it cannot be shown in the German sample.

Chinese Conceptualizations of Loyalty

The Chinese results provide only two employee loyalty reference objects. Table 6.3 shows the two factors emerging as reflective of loyalty to working group and loyalty to organization/supervisor. Chinese employees reflected organizational/supervisor loyalty as one combined reference object by wearing the company logo and promoting their supervisor's reputation externally to friends and internally to coworkers. Loyalty to their working teams was performed by engaging in the team as well as taking on extra group work. The results demonstrate that Chinese employees embody a BEL scale. (Note: These results have not been tested as extensively as other cultures and should be understood as a preliminary contribution to the final loyalty construct of the Eastern culture.)

The correlations of the Chinese sample in Table 6.4 are also interesting. Loyalty to working group, loyalty to organization, and the overall BEL scale

TABLE 6.3 Initial approach of employee loyalty concept for East Asian cultures (Exploratory Factor Analysis, Chinese sample)

Items	Factors	
	A. Loyalty to Working Group	B. Loyalty to Organization/ Supervisor
A Loyalty to Working Group		
1 I take an active part in my working group's affairs.	0.85	
2 I do more than one's share of the working group task.	0.82	
B Loyalty to Organization and Supervisor		
1 I tell my colleagues or friends about my supervisor's merits.		0.85
2 Also in my spare time I wear clothing (caps, jackets, lanyards, etc.) that bears the company's symbol or insignia (or I would do so if my company had such clothing).		0.75
Cronbach's alpha	0.59	0.47

Note
Loadings > 0.4 are reported, $N = 116$.

TABLE 6.4 Employee loyalty concept with negative outcomes (correlations, Chinese sample)

Variable	Mean	Standard Deviation	1	2	3
1 Loyalty to Working Group	5.83	0.89			
2 Loyalty to Organization/ Supervisor	5.06	1.20	0.19**		
3 BEL	5.45	0.82	0.56**	0.72**	
4 Work Overload	4.77	0.85	0.35**	0.16*	0.28**

Note
Kendall rank correlation method was applied, $N = 116$.
*Correlations are statistically significant at $p < 0.05$; **correlations are statistically significant at $p < 0.01$.

correlate strongly and significantly with each other. There is also a strong correlation of loyalty to work overload. The loyalty to working group seems to be an even greater risk with regard to work overload (0.35, $p < 0.01$) than the loyalty to organization/supervisor (0.16, $p < 0.05$). Hyper-loyal employees face the danger of work overload and are thus at risk of stress, burnout, and other negative health consequences.

Analysis

German and Chinese cultures perceive and perform loyalty differently in three key areas: defense, overwork, and the perception of supervisors within organizations.

Defense

China and Germany approach reference objects differently. German employees reflected traditional patterns of TEL typically found in Western cultures. Notable in this patterning are the direct and overt strategies that employees embrace to defend as a loyalty strategy. One reason for this can be seen in the historically comparatively weakly developed German conversation culture. In conversations, this means that Germans are easily perceived as rather pushy and insensitive in an international context. On the other hand, German directness is an expression of honesty and is therefore perceived as polite in Germany. Statements such as "I defend my organization when other employees criticize it," "I defend the honor of my working group whenever it is unfairly criticized," and "When somebody speaks ill of my supervisor, I will defend him/her immediately" (see Table 6.1) reflect true loyalty for Germans, but are not suitable for employees from an Eastern cultural background (see Table 6.3).

Eastern cultures are characterized by social harmony and face approach, so conflicts tend to be avoided or communicated indirectly. This is manifested in Chinese workplace culture. The intention to save face for other team members, particularly for supervisors, discourages employees from expressing their disagreements openly and directly. Rather, they are most likely to take actions for face-giving (to support the other person's need for inclusion and association) and face-assertion (to protect one's need for inclusion and association). Statements include "I tell my colleagues or friends about my supervisor's merits" and "Also in my spare time I wear clothing (caps, jackets, lanyards, etc.) that bears the company's symbol or insignia (or I would do so if my company had such clothing)" (see Table 6.3).

Overwork

Chinese participants expressed a higher willingness to work than German employees (e.g., "I do more than one's share of the working group task"). The unique cultural characteristics of Chinese workplace help to explain the willingness to take on more work or embrace the group identity. First, this finding speaks to the essentials of Confucian work ethics in Chinese companies. The dimension of "indulgence/restraint" offers insights looking into value orientation regarding work/life balance (Hofstede, 2011). It refers to the extent to which people try to control their desires and impulses. Chinese culture has a low score of 24 which demonstrates a restrained society in which people's actions are restricted by social norms. Employees, in general, are encouraged to work hard. In other words, work overload is regarded as a widely accepted social norm. Comparing with China, Germany culture scores 40 which has a low tendency towards the direction of controlling the gratification of their desires. Therefore, the tendency to overwork differs significantly in the two cultures.

What's more, this difference also relates to the concept of group orientation, which has been extensively examined in scholarly work on social values in Confucian societies (Pun, Chin, & Lau, 2000). As group interest outweighs individual interest, individuals are encouraged to sacrifice self-interest, such as spare time, for the good of the collective and company. Work overload is a commonly accepted norm in Chinese companies, as a way to demonstrate good work ethics and company loyalty.

Highly loyal Chinese employees would be more likely to give up their own free time and work–life balance in order to relieve colleagues of their workload. Loyal German employees, on the other hand, would be more likely to state the fact of overwork directly and communicate this to their manager. In Chinese culture, such behavior would be understood as direct criticism and violate the face approach. As a result, employees working overload usually would not ask for additional compensation. In some cases, employees would not even inform their supervisors openly and directly; instead, it is expected that supervisors and managers will discover and appraise the positive behaviors of their employees' work overload.

The behavior of work overload as a result of high employee loyalty is quite different in the two cultures and would also be managed differently. For instance, while work overload is interpreted as negative employee behavior in German companies, it is regarded very positively in Chinese companies. This illustrates why loyalty constructs cannot have universal validity and must be adapted to different cultural characteristics. Different cultural values and social norms embedded in the society as well as the corporate context could largely impact employee loyalty.

Perception of Supervisors

Chinese employees view the supervisor as the embodiment of the organization itself, rather than an individual in a power position, as is seen in German culture. Managers of Chinese companies are expected to be the "gentlemen" of Confucius who are caring, are moral, maintain their dignity, show wisdom, and are true to their word. As one of the most important features of Confucian values, *yi* ("righteousness") indicates, managers are expected to uphold high standards of moral conduct. They are regarded as the core spirit of the organization, particularly in traditional Chinese service-oriented industries, which are usually characterized by less formalized structures and processes. Instead of formalization of managerial practices, managers play crucial roles in directing and managing the growth of company, and those fundamental Confucian virtues invisibly govern employees' behaviors. In this sense, employees regard their supervisors and organization as a unit from a holistic perspective. Chinese employees' loyalty to their companies is largely demonstrated through their loyalty to supervisors.

In East Asian societies, Confucianism is rooted in humanistic values with an emphasis on personal ethics and morality. The five relationships of Confucianism are manifest in the managerial practices of Chinese companies. Those five relationships include loyalty between king and subject, relationship between father and son, duty between husband and wife, obedience to elders, and mutual trust between friends. At the core of those relationships stand five virtues: *ren* ("benevolence"), *yi* ("righteousness"), *li* ("propriety"), *zhi* ("wisdom"), and *xin* ("trustworthiness").

The importance of interpersonal relationships, known as *guanxi*, could further explain the positioning of supervisors as organizational representatives. For instance, interpersonal connections play a crucial role in business development, in particular expanding a business network and creating a favorable working environment (Cunningham & Rowley, 2010). Rather than promotion and monetary reward, in Chinese companies Confucian values motivate employees.

Employees' loyalty to their organization is manifested through their interpersonal connections and loyalty to their supervisors. In the context of Chinese companies, employees have developed loyalty to their supervisors over years spent in working relationships, and usually this type of working relationship extends to personal networks. Employees may get to meet and know the family members of their supervisors, and even become friends. This extension from working relationship to personal networks and friend circles is a typical feature of *guanxi* in Confucian culture, such as China, as there is no clear boundary. As a result, employees are more likely to develop strong loyalty to their supervisors and regard their supervisors and organizations as a unit; Chinese employees see their leaders as the embodiment of the organization (Zhang & Chen, 2013). During an organizational change in Chinese companies, for example, it is commonly observed that once an excellent leader or supervisor leaves, they may bring the whole team to the new organization.

Managerial Strategies

Employee loyalty is a complex psychological construct that is also subject to individual perceptions. Employee satisfaction, organizational commitment, and the psychological contract have a significant influence on loyalty. Although individual perceptions of these influencing factors cannot be determined with an authoritative quantitative study, they are of great importance. For example, if a supervisor cannot or will not keep promises to an employee, the employee's loyalty level will suffer. If the working group forms an emotional anchor for this employee, the loyalty to working group will be higher. Depending on whether the company's policy is perceived to support the negative behavior of the leader, the level of loyalty to organization will level off in the German culture. In Chinese culture, on the other hand, the supervisor and the company form a single unit. This would align with the Chinese cultural standard for strong interpersonal relationships and a hierarchy orientation. Due to these complex perceptions, it is very difficult to make universal statements about the loyalty of both Chinese and German employees.

In addition, we must consider the organizational contexts in which employees develop their loyalty over time. Organizational factors may play an important role, such as the size and type of organization, industry and sector, organizational history, core values, and organizational culture. While national cultural context matters the most, those cultural factors intersect with organizational factors that impact employee loyalty to a large extent. For instance, in state-owned companies or collective companies, there are usually strict hierarchies of management. This hierarchical structure leads to more close connections and interactions between line managers and supervisors with their subordinates, and as a result, employees may be more likely to develop high loyalty to their supervisors and regard their supervisors as the representatives of their organizations.

It is important to understand the cross-cultural differences in employee loyalty and their impact on negative behaviors. As discussed earlier, strong employee loyalty among Chinese employees is also defined by the tendency of higher work overload. It is up to interpersonally strong managers to recognize these negative tendencies, but this is more difficult in an increasingly global working world. Chinese and German employees and managers are increasingly working together and are often not sufficiently prepared for intercultural subtleties. German managers must therefore communicate very clearly to Chinese employees what behaviors they expect and what work commitment is to be understood as healthy and loyal. Conversely, Chinese managers should take into account the stronger individualism of German employees and also clearly communicate what behavior they believe reflects healthy loyalty.

Employee loyalty is a concept that is embedded in different cultural roots, and it has important practical implications for both managers and employees. Developing culturally appropriate understandings situated in sociocultural contexts is the first step for managers to cultivate their intercultural communication skills to effectively manage multicultural teams and organizations. In addition, management needs to be aware of the richness of employee loyalty from an intercultural perspective and develop diverse strategies to recognize and enhance employee loyalty to the organization.

Conclusion

This chapter offers fresh insights on employee loyalty from an intercultural perspective. Survey data collected from two service-oriented organizations in Germany and China clarifies the concept of loyalty as a multidimensional construct by identifying different reference objects and levels. While the empirical data collected from Germany supported a TEL scale, Chinese workers exhibited a BEL scale. Because employee loyalty is a concept derived from different cultural contexts, learning the cultural origins and roots could help to develop a more comprehensive understanding of the concept.

With an increase of intercultural interactions and communication at global workplace, developing culturally appropriate understandings of employee loyalty is key. From the managerial perspective, managers need to design necessary strategies and organizational procedures to support employee loyalty, as a way to better leverage employee loyalty as competitive advantage. From the perspective of employees, we suggest they develop cross-cultural understanding of employee loyalty and its relationship with workplace performance. Cultivating intercultural competence in multicultural teams and organizations is particularly relevant to understanding the increasing uncertainty and complexity in a globalized world.

Questions to Consider

- Why does employee loyalty differ in German and Chinese culture?
- Why does work overload not correlate with employee loyalty in Germany, but with employee loyalty in China?
- Do the cultural dimensions of power distance and individualism/collectivism provide a possible explanation?
- Which cultural standards have an influence on the negative behavior of work overload in the two cultures?
- What influence might the psychological contract have in each case?

Suggestions for Further Reading

Coughlan, R. (2005). Employee loyalty as adherence to shared moral values. *Journal of Managerial Issues*, 17(1), 43–57.

Hofstede, G. (2015). *6 dimensions for website*. Retrieved on August 10, 2022, from http://geerthofstede.com/research-and-vsm/dimension-data-matrix/

Meschke, S. (2021). *Employee loyalty: Intercultural comparison of European and East Asian approaches*. Cham: Springer Nature.

Rousseau, D. M., & Tijoriwala, S. A. (1998). Assessing psychological contracts: Issues, alternatives and measures. *Journal of Organizational Behavior*, 19(S1), 679–695.

Siegrist, J. (2001). A theory of occupational stress. In J. Dunham (Ed.), *Stress in workplace: Past, present and future* (pp. 52–66). London: Whurr Publishers.

References

Chen, Z. (2001). Further investigation of the outcomes of loyalty to supervisor: Job satisfaction and intention to stay. *Journal of Managerial Psychology*, 16(8), 650–660. https://doi.org/10.1108/EUM0000000006305

Coyle-Shapiro, J. A.-M., & Kessler, I. (2002). Exploring reciprocity through the lens of the psychological contract: Employee and employer perspectives. *European Journal of Work and Organizational Psychology*, 11(1), 1–18.

Cunningham, L. X., & Rowley, C. (2010). Small and medium-sized enterprises in China: A literature review, human resource management and suggestions for further research. *Asia Pacific Business Review*, 16(3), 319–337.

De Vos, A., Buyens, D., & Schalk, R. (2003). Psychological contract development during organizational socialization: Adaptation to reality and the role of reciprocity. *Journal of Organizational Behavior*, 24(5), 537–559.

Herriot, P., & Pemberton, C. (1997). Facilitating new deals. *Human Resource Management Journal*, 7(1), 45–56.

Hofstede, G. (2011). Dimensionalizing cultures: The Hofstede model in context. *Online Readings in Psychology and Culture*, 2(1), 2307-0919.

Hofstede, G. (2015). *6 dimensions for website*. Retrieved on August 10, 2022, from http://geerthofstede.com/research-and-vsm/dimension-data-matrix/

James, K., & Cropanzano, R. (1994). Dispositional group loyalty and individual action for the benefit of an ingroup: Experimental and correlational evidence. *Organizational Behavior and Human Decision Processes*, 60(2), 179– 205. https://doi.org/10.1006/obhd.1994.1080

Luchak, A. A. (2003). What kind of voice do loyal employees use? *British Journal of Industrial Relations*, 41(1), 115–134.

Meschke, S. (2021). *Employee loyalty: Intercultural comparison of European and East Asian approaches*. Cham: Springer Nature.

Pun, K. F., Chin, K. S., & Lau, H. (2000). A review of the Chinese cultural influences on Chinese enterprise management. *International Journal of Management Reviews*, 2(4), 325–338.

Siegrist, J., Starke, D., Chandola, T., Godin, I., Marmot, M., Niedhammer, I., & Peter, R. (2004). The measurement of effort-reward imbalance at work: European comparisons. *Social Science & Medicine*, 58(8), 1483–1499.

Tabarsa, G. A., Tehrani, M., Lotfi, N., Ahadian, M., Baniasadi, A., & Tabarsa, E. (2013). Leisure time management: A new approach toward employees loyalty. *Journal of Management and Strategy*, 4(3), 65–80.

Thompson, J. A., & Bunderson, J. S. (2003). Violations of principle: Ideological currency in the psychological contract. *Academy of Management Review, 28*(4), 571–586.

Yee, R. W. Y., Yeung, A. C. L., & Cheng, T. C. E. (2010). An empirical study of employee loyalty, service quality and firm performance in the service industry. *International Journal of Production Economics, 24*(1), 109–120.

Zhang, Y., & Chen, C. C. (2013). Developmental leadership and organizational citizenship behavior: Mediating effects of self-determination, supervisor identification, and organizational identification. *The Leadership Quarterly, 24*(4), 534–543.

7
LEVERAGING CULTURE TO CONFRONT SEXUAL HARASSMENT IN A MULTICULTURAL ORGANIZATION

Amy Grim Buxbaum and Mara K. Berkland

The 2017 #MeToo movement focused public awareness on the persistent and pervasive problem of sexual harassment. In the wake of high-profile scandals in the American entertainment industry, the news was filled with stories of sexual harassment and assault in politics, education, media, the military, nonprofits, and across business sectors. In the wake of #MeToo, many organizations were compelled to examine their policies and practices, but given the systemic and multifaceted nature of the problem, it has proven to be difficult to address (Kantor, 2018). Unfortunately, sexual harassment persists in business, and indeed in workplaces of all kinds, despite recent gains in public awareness and public support for the movement (Brown, 2022; Holman & Kalmoe, 2021). Sexual harassment remains a complicated and vexing issue that professionals, especially women, are likely to encounter directly or indirectly during their career in some way, whether as a victim, a target, a bystander, a supervisor, a coworker, or a close colleague of someone who is affected. Understanding organizational policies and cultural norms that influence the experience and adjudication of sexual harassment should be of concern to every ethical professional in today's global workplace.

This chapter examines a unique workplace in the Netherlands where employees from diverse national cultural backgrounds responded to an alleged incident of sexual harassment in their organization. The case shows how members of a multinational team leveraged their knowledge of their organization's national host culture in order to create a message that is critical of management and simultaneously establishes its own legitimacy to speak on the complex and difficult issue of sexual harassment. Their formal response to organizational statements illustrates the ways multinational employee teams can harness the cultural values of their company to advocate for change.

Sexual Harassment

Although people can be harassed in a sexual or gender-based way in all kinds of settings, sexual harassment is generally understood to be a workplace phenomenon in that it is tied to conditions of employment. In other words, the workplace or employment context is what makes such behavior meet the definition of sexual harassment. Legally, the concept of sexual harassment developed through lawsuits brought under the U.S. Civil Rights Act of 1964 and subsequent federal labor laws which prohibit employment discrimination based on race, sex, gender, religion, or other protected classes. Today, the U.S. Equal Employment Opportunity Commission explains sexual harassment this way:

> It is unlawful to harass a person (an applicant or employee) because of that person's sex. Harassment can include "sexual harassment" or unwelcome sexual advances, requests for sexual favors, and other verbal or physical harassment of a sexual nature.
> Harassment does not have to be of a sexual nature, however, and can include offensive remarks about a person's sex. For example, it is illegal to harass a woman by making offensive comments about women in general.
> Both victim and the harasser can be either a woman or a man, and the victim and harasser can be the same sex.
> Although the law doesn't prohibit simple teasing, offhand comments, or isolated incidents that are not very serious, harassment is illegal when it is so frequent or severe that it creates a hostile or offensive work environment or when it results in an adverse employment decision (such as the victim being fired or demoted).
> The harasser can be the victim's supervisor, a supervisor in another area, a co-worker, or someone who is not an employee of the employer, such as a client or customer.

The United States was one of the first countries to codify sexual harassment into law in the 1980s, and the U.S. law has served as a "legal transplant" that has been adapted by many other legal systems around the world (Asmaat & Mehboob, 2016). In 1992, the United Nations Committee on the Elimination of Discrimination against Women developed the following definition, which also highlights the workplace setting:

> Sexual harassment includes such unwelcome sexually determined behaviour as physical contact and advances, sexually coloured remarks,

showing pornography and sexual demands, whether by words or actions. Such conduct can be humiliating and may constitute a health and safety problem; it is discriminatory when the woman has reasonable ground to believe that her objection would disadvantage her in connection with her employment, including recruitment or promotion, or when it creates a hostile working environment.

In sum, sexual harassment refers to a range of unwelcome sexual behaviors in professional and workplace settings. It can occur verbally, nonverbally, physically, online, or through electronic communication. Typically, it involves a power dynamic in which one person holds a position of organizational power or authority that may influence the employment conditions of another and, as such, is seen as an abuse of power.

Sexual Harassment across the Globe

A recent Gallup survey finds that "workplace violence and harassment are widespread phenomena throughout the world," with more than one in five employees reporting that they have personally experienced some form of violence or harassment at work (Crabtree, 2022). The first-of-its-kind global survey queried 74,000 workers in 121 countries about a range of harassing and violent behavior, such as workplace bullying, but specifically with regard to sexual violence and harassment, 6% of employed people had experienced such behavior at work, including 8% of women and 5% of men. Although this percentage is much lower than other sources report (see Asmaat & Mehboob, 2016; Berryman-Fink, 2001), it equates to more than 200 million people worldwide. Still, 6% is likely an underestimate, given that these kinds of cases are notoriously underreported. Only about half of victims reported they had ever told anyone about their experience, primarily because they perceived that doing so would be a "waste of time" or would negatively impact their reputation, or because reporting procedures were unclear (Crabtree, 2022).

Complicating matters on a global scale, countries have distinctive legal systems that define and sanction sexual harassment differently. Although sexual harassment law originated in the United States, it has been adopted to some degree by many countries internationally "with differing results as each nation has drawn on its own legal and cultural traditions to fashion its own approach" (Asmaat & Mehboob, 2016, p. 37). Because cultures may have diverse codes, norms, values, and ideologies with regard to gender roles and sexuality, it makes sense that cultural orientations would influence the occurrence, tolerance, and consequences for such behavior (see Luthar & Luthar, 2007). In a cross-cultural study examining reactions to sexual harassment, for example, Sigal and Jacobsen (1999) found distinct cultural differences in tolerance of sexual harassment, perceptions about the credibility of victims, attitudes toward punishment, and the potential for rehabilitation. Otterbach, Sousa-Poza and Zhang (2021) found that perceptions of workplace harassment are tied to cultural assumptions about gender equality. Other recent studies have explored media framing of the #MeToo movement in different countries including Sweden (Pollack, 2019), Jordan (Al-Mahadin, 2019), and Russia and Japan (Kasianenko, 2019). Altogether, it is clear that although the movement may have helped to increase awareness worldwide, sexual harassment has very different manifestations in different cultures.

As organizations become increasingly global, understanding the cultural norms and nuances regarding potentially harassing behavior becomes imperative for global professionals. Conduct that might be seen as normal, or at least tolerated, in one culture may be seen as highly problematic in another culture (Luthar & Luthar, 2007). This not only affects individuals who may be involved in a potentially harassing situation and organizational leaders who must craft sound policy, but it also affects organizations at the departmental and group levels. In multicultural workplaces where employees from different cultures interact, cases of purported sexual harassment might present occasions where cultural norms and values are made visible and open to question.

Cultural Context: A Multicultural Organization

The artifacts for this analysis come from a multinational organization founded and based in the Netherlands. This mid-sized company has offices worldwide and employs professionals from around the globe, many of whom work in multicultural departments with colleagues from several different cultures.

The national context of this company, the Netherlands, is relatively average, or in the center, of the power distance dimension. The power distance dimension measures the degree of inequality which people in a population feel is acceptable. On that scale, the Netherlands scores 38, which means that the Dutch generally value personal independence, hierarchy as a facilitator of efficiency, visibility, accessible managers who coach rather than command, and decision-making by consensus (Hofstede, 2022; Hofstede & Soeters, 2002). A priority of egalitarian-leaning cultures is to create psychological safety within organizations, which is crucial to free exchange. The intentional shrinking of power distance creates a safe space where organizational or team members can connect (Batt-Rawden & Traavik, 2022).

Additionally, the Dutch people operate from a low-context orientation. Most relevant for this case is that disagreement is often depersonalized in low-context cultures. Logic and rational perspectives are prioritized, and communication is seen as a transparent tool to convey that rationality. Unlike high-context leaning cultures, where significant emphasis is placed on nonverbal elements and prioritizing harmony, low-context orientations focus on denotative messages (Gudykunst & Ting-Toomey, 1988; Levitt, 2022; Oetzel et al., 2012). To illustrate, the mission of the organization in this case underscores this cultural orientation in its mission statement, which attests its commitment to creating an environment that is "open, honest, inclusive and supportive" where fairness and dignity are ensured.

Cultural Artifact: Email Exchange about Allegations of Sexual Harassment

The messages below are part of an email exchange among employees who work in the same functional unit. This Dutch-based multicultural department includes professionals from a wide range of countries, including the Netherlands, the United States, Spain, Turkey, Ireland, Belgium, and India. The emails pertain to accusations of sexual harassment in which a well-known senior male member of their department was accused of misconduct toward a female junior team member from a different department.[1] The following analysis focuses primarily on the team response in email #3, but since it responds to and even directly draws from the first two messages, we have included them here for context.

BOX 7.1   EMAIL #1: TEAM LEADER'S INITIAL EMAIL TO THE DEPARTMENT

From a lead female employee in the accused male's department:

> I would like to inform you of an interaction. Friday it came to my attention rumors regarding an incident between two employees asserting that [female] was approached by [male] in a way that is not professionally suitable.
>
> We take these allegations very seriously. A safe working environment for everyone is a priority for [company name]. We investigated and concluded that [female's] claims were 100% lies. Furthermore, the false rumors have been circulating for months, which I find very disturbing.

> We take this very seriously and are deliberating on next steps. We cannot allow people to harm their colleagues and jeopardize their careers. Should you hear such stories and have any concerns, you should always contact HR or me. We will then investigate what happened and take the appropriate actions to prevent lies from being spread either internally or outside our organization.
>
> Me and [HR representative] are available in case you should have questions or concerns.

BOX 7.2   EMAIL #2: MANAGER'S FOLLOW-UP MESSAGE TO THE DEPARTMENT

Email #2: Manager's Follow-Up Message to the Department

From a manager in the accused male's department:

> Hi team, I would like to share/inform you about the email that was written and sent today by [female department lead] to the [department] team. This is an important issue, one which we hope you have not had to experience or witness. If you find yourself in such a situation or see/hear about somebody else being in such a situation, please let me, [office supervisors] or [head of HR] from HR know.

BOX 7.3   EMAIL #3: TEAM MEMBERS' RESPONSE

Email #3: Team Members' Response

From a lead female employee in the accused male's department:

> As a multinational team coming from diverse backgrounds, we feel compelled to make a clear and unified statement regarding our reactions to the recent misconduct rumors, subsequent handling by leadership, and our expectations moving forward.
>
> Firstly, we will focus on the subject of our working environment. Through communications sent on [date], direct harm was done to the named individuals in this situation, and, more broadly, to anyone who may

wish to speak out. Naming the accuser in any communication creates an unsafe environment for employees and a compounding, chilling effect for anyone who may wish to name a harassment or misconduct perpetrator. In several of our team's home countries, this is not only a breach of workplace norms, but also the law. The consequence to our staff is a direct contradiction to the very values -- discretion and fairness -- [company] leadership asked its employees to uphold during the handling of this situation.

We would also like to address the veiled and unspecific language implying the accuser did not take the appropriate interventions. The communications shared to date, by both leadership and HR, do not outline how accusations should be reported. Moreover, they have not recognized the realities of power imbalance victims are known to face. Rarely do such situations start so obviously. It should not be up to the victim to decode the proper way to escalate an accusation. That responsibility lies with the organization and individuals in power.

Further, phrasing like "100% lies" or "heeft verteld 100% gelogen" puts the responsibility on the victim to prove someone behaved inappropriately towards them. Language like this empowers individuals who would commit harassment, knowing that recipients will ultimately have trouble proving allegations. Also, we would point out that there is a lack of broad transparency around the process [the company] uses to uncover the truthfulness of allegations and how and when consequences are applied. The result is that victims do not know the company supports them and may, understandably, expect the agency to uphold the status quo of long-known and problematic power dynamics.

Several team members who have been at [company] for a longer time noted there has been an increased awareness given to these kinds of issues, however, a sustainable, adequate solution has not been found. The emails sent did not recognize the nuance or complexity of the issue. It was clear the mandated company training sessions and policies that followed similar incidents did not prevent this most recent situation, revealing the long-identified deeper seeded cultural problem has not yet been fixed. We do not see this as a result of one person's mistake or individual action. It went through multiple people, each of whom could have identified it as inappropriate or a sensitive issue that required oversight from HR or legal. Our team feels especially disappointed because we believe in [company], and it is deeply disheartening when we see repeated issues, lack of responsibility for the problem, and an inadequate response. Particularly the solution of coming to the office to talk with [senior company and HR leaders] felt disconnected from our new WFH norm and does not ensure the problem isn't repeated in the future.

> Our expectation is that [company] works to restore a safe working environment for employees of all genders, orientations, and backgrounds. In order to do this, we propose the following:
>
> 1. We as a team would like [company] to provide a clear and transparent process for how accusations are to be investigated and what consequences may be applied.
> 2. Second, in an effort to restore trust, we request assurance that both parties were treated fairly during this process, that they are now being cared for and steps are being taken to ensure they are ok.
> 3. Lastly, we respect that we are all continuously developing our understanding of how to handle these situations so we would like an acknowledgment of these issues and a direct, clear statement of support from leadership for victims or accusers, recognizing the immense burden they carry. In the long term, we would like to see more sustainable solutions such as a role dedicated to determining how these issues should be handled on a case-to-case basis.
>
> The communications shared on [date] have done significant damage to our trust and our perception that [company] offers a safe work environment. We as a team collectively ask that leadership takes pains to unwind that damage and restore safe working conditions with clear and immediate action. We are not asking for perfection but requesting significant and decisive progress.
>
> Sincerely,
> [multinational team member names]

Clearly, the team was displeased with management's messages, but more than being a disagreement about the company's handling of the allegations, there are subtle yet discernable nuances in play that help to explain the team's response from a cultural perspective. Although the team behind the email was not primarily Dutch, in several ways they drew from their company's Dutch cultural orientation to legitimize their claims and to call for organizational improvement.

Analysis: Leveraging Culture to Establish Legitimacy

In order to unpack the cultural undercurrents of this email exchange among members of this multicultural department, we employed critical discourse analysis. Critical discourse analysis is a theoretical and methodological approach that examines the ways that discourse (i.e., communication) recreates social rules. In this view, discourse both reflects and reinforces social norms in the ways it frames or advocates for certain perspectives. This method is used in a variety of areas, including studies of organization and management (Vaara & Tienar, 2008; Vaara, Tienar, & Koveshnikov, 2021). Critical discourse analysis prompts scholars to closely examine the micro-level elements of concrete messages, such as these emails, as instances of larger discourses. The critical nature of this approach prompts the analyst to look closely at what is assumed or which ideologies and values are tied to the codes and how power differences are replicated (Fairclough, 2010; van Dijk, 1998).

One way power is negotiated is through establishing who has legitimate standing to speak about certain issues. In organizations, legitimacy is tied to organizational roles and responsibilities that correspond to positions in the structural hierarchy, but legitimacy can also be claimed and constructed communicatively. Legitimacy can be defined as what is proper and just, or that which embodies the values of what is proper (Sillince & Brown, 2009), and what is proper is culturally defined. One strategy for gaining or creating legitimacy is by using the tools of the audience or the empowered group to craft an argument (Suddaby & Greenwood, 2005). In other words, by "speaking the language" of those in power, one can attempt to demonstrate the rightfulness of one's own position by showing how it is consistent with the dominant cultural perspective.

The international team who penned the letter of concern to company management in email #3 drew from the company's dominant Dutch culture in order to illustrate the contradictions in institutional logics and to justify their own position. The performance of legitimacy is seen in a number of phrases that point out the ways that the company disregarded expectations of safety, as well as of equality and fairness, which are key values of the company and of Dutch culture. Furthermore, they do so using low-context-oriented statements which, for many cultures, could be considered confrontational and consequently disrespectful and disruptive to team or organizational harmony, but which are more acceptable in the low-context Dutch culture.

Safety

One contradiction involves the conceptualization of a safe workplace. For example, email #1 assured that "a safe working environment for everyone is a priority" for management and later states that "we cannot allow people to harm their colleagues and jeopardize their careers." At first glance, this might seem to be an appropriate response to sexual harassment, but a closer look reveals that the harm highlighted is not sexual harassment per se, but rather is the accusation. Notice how "harm" is embedded between statements about "100% lies," "false rumors," and "such stories." The penultimate sentence underscores this point explicitly: "We will then investigate what happened and take the appropriate actions to prevent lies from being spread either internally or outside our organization." In this construction, being safe is equated with not being wrongfully accused.

The team picks up on this language of "safety" email #3, but its meaning is different. Early on, the employees note, "Naming the accuser in any communication creates an *unsafe* environment for employees and a compounding, chilling effect for anyone who may wish to name a harassment or misconduct perpetrator" (emphasis added). Here, the team uses the language of safety to point out how the management's actions undermine the safety of potential victims by creating a communicative climate that discourages reporting for fear of being publicly named and shamed by management. Later the team further attempts to reclaim "safety" by stating "Our expectation is that [company] works to restore a safe working environment for employees," which is followed by a number of specific requests.

While management's email focuses on the safety of the accused, the employees emphasize the safety of all parties, seeking assurances "that they are now being cared for and steps are being taken to ensure they are ok." In closing, the team reiterates that management's messages "have done significant damage to our trust and our perception that [company] offers a safe work environment" and calls on the company to "restore safe working conditions with clear and immediate action." Throughout their response, the employees attempt to legitimate their position by employing the language of safety introduced by management, but by expanding its definition in the ways that hold the organization to account not only for its initial email but also for its policies regarding the reporting and investigation of claims of sexual harassment. Drawing attention to management's prioritization of the reputation of high-ranking organizational members (in this case, a male one) highlights the antithetical values of power and safety, especially when it comes to sexual harassment. When rules are not applied equally, or when processes are structured to allow some organizational members more voice than others, psychological safety is compromised. Highlighting how the hierarchy is threatening the psychological safety of lower-ranking organizational members is an effective deployment of the Dutch power distance orientation.

Fairness and Dignity

In addition, the team simultaneously challenges and bolsters Dutch cultural values in its call for fairness and dignity for all parties, including the accuser. One way it does so is by highlighting its own multicultural composition as grounds for its own legitimacy. For instance, the team underscores its multiculturality in questioning management's actions while at the same time naming company and Dutch cultural norms:

> In several of our team's home countries, this [naming the accuser] is not only a breach of workplace norms, but also the law. The consequence to our staff is a direct contradiction to the very values — discretion and fairness — [company] leadership asked its employees to uphold during the handling of this situation.

Moreover, pointing out that the actions of leadership were so egregious as to break the law in many of the writers' home countries gives the team a position of moral authority. Emphasizing that the writers come from countries with codified protections for the disempowered frames the inequity of the Dutch leadership team as anachronistic and patriarchal. While summoning their home countries to point out a different approach to handling sensitive issues of sexual harassment, the team at the same time emphasizes the company's Dutch value of fairness. Specifically, the team holds management responsible for enacting these values in cases of sexual harassment—management should be held to the same standards as they are asking of employees. By pointing out how management contradicts the stated values of "discretion and fairness" by outing the accuser, they undermine the legitimacy of leadership in this situation specifically and surrounding issues of sexual harassment more generally.

Equality

The team's email also speaks to the cultural value of equality by calling attention to the inherent power imbalance. The team underscores the greater power management has, even within a strongly egalitarian culture, to communicate what is or is not acceptable behavior in the workplace. Not only is management in a position of authority to publicly name the parties, the act of doing so influences the communicative environment. In paragraph three, the team states:

> Moreover, they [management's messages] have not recognized the realities of power imbalance victims are known to face. Rarely do such situations start so obviously. It should not be up to the victim to decode the proper way to escalate an accusation. That responsibility lies with the organization and individuals in power.

This statement draws attention to the fact that leadership created a barrier to equity, rather than opening access to due process as their organizational and national culture would expect. The fact that the team recognizes this and points it out seemingly without regard for face provides them, and their way of interacting, legitimacy. They continue this theme when they denounce more language from the original email and say, "Further, phrasing like '100% lies' or 'heeft verteld 100% gelogen' puts the responsibility on the victim." Language like this empowers individuals who would commit harassment, knowing that recipients will ultimately have trouble proving allegations. The clear identification of the lopsided burden of proof emphasizes the lack of equal due process.

The team's response not only reminds its readers of the power imbalance that existed in the interaction, but in the failure of the organization to mitigate inquiries that are unrelated to job responsibilities, a concept that egalitarian leaning cultures understand. Midway through the response, the team's message shifts to a more aggressive tactic for centering its voice as *the* legitimate moral authority. At the end of paragraph four, the team reminds leadership that the company has a history of "long-known and problematic power dynamics" and moves on to assert that this problem, despite having been discussed and prioritized, has not been adequately addressed by the organization and violates the values that the organization purports to hold: "mandated company training sessions and policies that followed similar incidents did not prevent this most recent situation, revealing the long-identified deeper seeded cultural problem has not yet been fixed." The employee response preempts any scapegoating by clarifying: "We do not see this as a result of one person's mistake or individual action. It went through multiple people, each of whom could have identified it as inappropriate or a sensitive issue that required oversight from HR or legal," emphasizing the historical embedded norms of the organization are so entrenched that the system itself cannot be trusted.

After they delegitimize organizational values and leadership, the employee response shifts to its specific recommendations by turning to another priority, low-context communication, as part of the solution to bringing the culture in line with organizational and cultural values. Their recommendations focus on clarity and transparency of communication, pointing out the second value disregarded in company interaction, directness that dispassionately addresses conflict. Overall, the team's response is direct and clear and even rather confrontational, seemingly without regard to management's face needs or deferring to their authority. High-context cultures find public disagreements threatening because they risk causing embarrassment or loss of face, but members of low-context cultures are more capable of detaching the conflict problems from the people involved. As a consequence, direct, logic-focused, explicit communication codes are expected and appreciated in low-context cultures (Croucher et al, 2012; Ting-Toomey, 1985). In this way, the team email is written within the parameters of the company's dominant Dutch culture.

In the end, the response by the employees calls into question the moral legitimacy of the organization. Calling into question the equity and clarity embedded in the "organization's outputs, procedures, structures, and leaders" (Castelló & Lozano, 2011, p. 13), the team asserts its own multicultural voice in ways that are consistent with the company's national culture. Having argued that the organization has not done the right thing based on Dutch values as well as the standards of their own cultures, the response positions itself as the authority to which the organizational leadership must account. The team's legitimacy is demonstrated in the ways the team response marries the ideologies of context orientation and equality, which are sometimes in tension. The team develops a position of legitimacy by highlighting how the organization has missed the balancing of the two competing perspectives. The multicultural team leans on Dutch norms and performs them better than the organizational superintendents, who, by virtue of their levels of responsibility, would be expected to embody and perform the shared values and ideologies more adroitly.

Conclusion

This case shows how members of a multinational team within a Dutch organization harnessed their knowledge of their organization's national host culture in order to create a message that is critical of management and simultaneously establishes its own legitimacy to speak on the complex and difficult issue of sexual harassment. Multinational teams in workplaces inspire organizations to be more inclusive of diverse perspectives, but they often must also work within the parameters of the dominant culture in order to be taken seriously. Management is more likely to embrace such exchanges when the result is improved performance, but less likely to do so when the discourse is at odds with the organizational values or structure. The team here used its multicultural positioning alongside its specific cultural knowledge to register its concerns in a culturally sanctioned way, thereby increasing its chances of being heard and considered by management.

Discussion Questions

- Why do you think victims of sexual harassment are reluctant to report harassing behavior? In what kinds of cultural orientations would you expect victims to be more likely to report? Less likely to report? Why?

- How is the accusation framed by organizational leaders? What words are used? What values or worldviews does the email from the accused department's email reflect and reinforce?
- How is the accusation framed by team members? What words are used? What values or worldviews does the email from the accused department's email reflect and reinforce?
- How might values or worldviews surrounding hierarchy/egalitarianism impact the potential occurrences of sexual harassment in the workplace?
- Why might multinational teams feel more or less comfortable countering cultural norms?

Note

1 This exchange is based on actual correspondence that took place in the company that was shared by a participant in the exchange. The messages have been edited to remove any potentially identifying information. The original correspondence occurred in both Dutch and English languages, depending on the writer of the email, and we have translated it all to English here.

Suggestions for Further Reading

Crabtree, S. (2022, December 14). Global study: 23% of workers experience violence, harassment. *Gallup.* https://news.gallup.com/opinion/gallup/406793/global-study-workers-experience-violence-harassment.aspx

Kantor, J. (2018, March 23). #MeToo called for an overhaul: Are workplaces really changing? *New York Times.* https://www.nytimes.com/2018/03/23/us/sexual-harassment-workplace-response.html

Keyton, J., Clair, R., Compton, C. A., Dougherty, D. S., Forbes Berthoud, D., Manning, J., & Scarduzio, J. A. (2018). Addressing sexual harassment in a sexually charged national culture: A Journal of Applied Communication Research forum. *Journal of Applied Communication Research, 46,* 665–683.

Luthar, H. K., & Luthar, V. K. (2007). A theoretical framework explaining cross-cultural sexual harassment: Integrating Hofstede and Schwartz. *Journal of Labor Research, 28*(1), 169–188.

U.S. Equal Employment Opportunity Commission (2022, April). *Sexual harassment in our nation's workplaces.* https://www.eeoc.gov/data/sexual-harassment-our-nations-workplaces#_ftnref3

References

Al-Mahadin, S. (2019). Real Jordanian women don't get harassed: Mapping sexual harassment along ultra-nationalist lines. *International Journal of Media & Cultural Politics, 15,* 381–384.

Asmaat, R., & Mehboob, M. S. (2016). International laws and policies for addressing sexual harassment in the workplace. *International Research Journal of Interdisciplinary & Multidisciplinary Studies, II*(II), 32–43.

Batt-Rawden, V. H., & Traavik, L. E. M. (2022). Fostering egalitarianism for team learning in professional service teams. *The Learning Organization, 29*, 597–614. https://doi.org/10.1108/TLO-01-2022-0007

Berryman-Fink, C. (2001). Women's responses to sexual harassment at work: Organizational policy versus employee practice. *Employment Relations Today, 27*(4), 57–64.

Brown, A. (2022). More than twice as many Americans support than oppose the #MeToo movement. *Pew Research Center.* https://www.pewresearch.org/social-trends/2022/09/29/more-than-twice-as-many-americans-support-than-oppose-the-metoo-movement/

Castelló, I., & Lozano, J. M. (2011). Searching for new forms of legitimacy through corporate responsibility rhetoric. *Journal of Business Ethics, 100*, 11–29.

Crabtree, S. (2022, December 14). Global study: 23% of workers experience violence, harassment. *Gallup.* https://news.gallup.com/opinion/gallup/406793/global-study-workers-experience-violence-harassment.aspx

Croucher, S. M., Bruno, A., McGrath, P., Adams, C., McGahan, C., Suits, A., & Huckins, A. (2012). Conflict styles and high–low context cultures: A cross-cultural extension. *Communication Research Reports, 29*(1), 64–73.

Fairclough, N. (2010). *Critical discourse analysis: The critical study of language.* Harlow: Longman.

Gudykunst, W. B., & Ting-Toomey, S. (1988). *Culture and interpersonal communication.* Newbury Park, CA: Sage.

Hofstede, G. (2022). The Netherlands. *Hofstede Insights.* https://www.hofstede-insights.com/fi/product/compare-countries/

Hofstede, G., & Soeters, J. (2002). Consensus societies with their own character: National cultures in Japan and the Netherlands. *Comparative Sociology, 1*(1), 1–16.

Holman, M., & Kalmoe, N. P. (2021). The polls—trends: Sexual harassment. *Public Opinion Quarterly, 85*, 706–718.

Kantor, J. (2018, March 23). #MeToo called for an overhaul: Are workplaces really changing? *The New York Times.* https://www.nytimes.com/2018/03/23/us/sexual-harassment-workplace-response.html

Kasianenko, K. (2019). When is it us too? How Russian and Japanese media framed sexual harassment towards their journalists. *Interactions: Studies in Communication & Culture, 10*, 201–221.

Levitt, S. R. (2022). Intercultural competence in international teamwork: Understanding high-and low-context communication styles. *Communication and Media in Asia Pacific, 5*(1), 1–13. http://doi.org/10.14456/cmap.2022.1

Luthar, H. K., & Luthar, V. K. (2007). A theoretical framework explaining cross-cultural sexual harassment: Integrating Hofstede and Schwartz. *Journal of Labor Research, 28*(1), 169–188.

Oetzel, J. G., McDermott, V. M., Torres, A., & Sanchez, C. (2012). The impact of individual differences and group diversity on group interaction climate and satisfaction: A test of the effective intercultural workgroup communication theory. *Journal of International and Intercultural Communication, 5*(2), 144–167.

Otterbach, S., Sousa-Poza, A., & Zhang, X. (2021). Gender differences in perceived workplace harassment and gender egalitarianism: A comparative cross-national analysis. *Business Ethics, the Environment & Responsibility, 30*, 392–411.

Pollack, E. (2019). Sweden and the #MeToo movement. *Interactions: Studies in Communication & Culture, 10,* 185–200.

Sigal, J., & Jacobsen, H. (1999). A cross-cultural exploration of factors affecting reactions to sexual harassment. *Psychology, Public Policy, and Law, 5,* 760–785.

Sillince, J. A., & Brown, A. D. (2009). Multiple organizational identities and legitimacy: The rhetoric of police websites. *Human Relations, 62*(12), 1829–1856.

Suddaby, R., & Greenwood, R. (2005). Rhetorical strategies of legitimacy. *Administrative Science Quarterly, 50*(1), 35–67.

Ting-Toomey, S. (1985). Toward a theory of conflict and culture. In W. B. Gudykunst, L. P. Stewart & S. Ting-Toomey (Eds.), *Communication, culture, and organizational processes* (pp. 71–86). Beverly Hills, CA: Sage.

United Nations Committee on the Elimination of Discrimination Against Women, Eleventh Session (1992, January). *General recommendation No. 19: Violence against women.* United Nations Human Rights Office of the High Commissioner. https://www.ohchr.org/en/treaty-bodies/cedaw/general-recommendations

U.S. Equal Employment Opportunity Commission (n.d.). *Sexual harassment.* https://www.eeoc.gov/sexual-harassment

Vaara, E., & Tienar, J. (2008). A discursive perspective on legitimation strategies in multinational corporations. *Academy of Management Review, 33*(4), 985–993.

Vaara, E., Tienar, J., & Koveshnikov, A. (2021). From cultural differences to identity politics: A critical discursive approach to national identity in multinational corporations. *Journal of Management Studies, 58*(8), 2052–2081.

van Dijk, T. A. (1998). *Ideology.* London: Sage.

PART 3
Institutional Contexts

8
CULTURAL TOURISM AND RETAIL STORE AESTHETICS IN NORWAY AND MOROCCO

Mara K. Berkland

Tourism is an increasingly lucrative industry especially for developing markets, and businesses that cater to global travelers need to understand and adapt to their customers. The complex needs of buyers in a global marketplace must be considered through the lens of culture, which offers an additional worldview dimension that extends beyond the consumption expectations of familiar demographic groupings. For countries that specialize in *cultural tourism*, which is associated with a particular destination and its cultural elements such as traditions, history, lifestyle, handicrafts, food, religion, and clothing, translating host cultural values to the visiting culture becomes especially important.

Tourism and shopping are often synonymous, and for many tourists, shopping is the purpose, if not the proof, of having traveled (Law & Au, 2000; Timothy, 2005). Souvenirs that reflect elements of culture often become emblematic of the travelers' experiences. The amount of money spent shopping while traveling internationally is often more than the cost of lodging and food, so the ability to sell products to tourists is critical to local economies. Purveyors of traditional wares understand that creating a circumstance where their cultural goods are desirable to foreigners is key to both their individual financial success and the prosperity of the tourist destination community. Substantial monetary support is infused into local economies by shopping tourism (Murphy et al., 2011; Yüksel, 2004).

Anticipating tourists' shopping preferences, styles, and aesthetics is complicated by the sheer number of different national cultures a tourist destination may attract. Each one of those cultures may have different travel motivations as well as preferences for tourism products and services.

DOI: 10.4324/9781003298199-12

Some craftspeople and merchants are capable of aesthetically suiting the evolving needs of the tourist market, creating success for themselves, and then being able to make more diverse and complex cultural adaptations and teaching their peers how to similarly adjust. When successful, these product and service adjustments take into account the particular patterns of tourist behaviors, which reflect the values and worldview orientations of the visitors.

Cultural Values and Souvenirs

Cultural values provide a structure to decide the norms and symbols to be embraced in particular contexts, including the shaping of lifestyles, spending habits, and product choices. As a consequence, retail aesthetics such as signage, product design, packaging, and store layout tend to reflect the values of the producing culture. When cultural tourists shop, they are aware of and anticipate a degree of difference from their own cultures. They often embrace the novel elements that will remind them of the experiences they enjoyed while immersing in a different culture.

In many ways, cultural tourists are ideal consumers of cultural goods because they exhibit a curiosity and interest in customs and products unlike their own. However, that interest is always mitigated by their own cultural bias. Tourists, in their behavior and in their consumption, negotiate the tensions of familiarity and novelty (Cohen, 1972). Familiarity is reflected in a tourist's need for home comforts, whether it be food, aspects of living accommodations, or language translators. Novelty manifests in their desire to connect with new ideas, flavors, and stories. As consumers, they vary in their tolerance for newness, their need for home comforts, and their desire to interact with locals outside of the tourist industry. Their need for novelty brings them to the foreign location and makes them eager to adapt, at least to a degree. But, while it goes without saying that their desire for novelty is much higher than their compatriots who choose to vacation within their own cultural borders, complete novelty is still uncomfortable.

Uncertainty Avoidance Dimension of Culture

Some cultural dimensions become more important in certain contexts, and in the case of international retail interactions, the dimension of uncertainty avoidance is one of the most significant. The negotiation of the need for familiarity and the desire for novelty influences tourists' expectations and decision-making. It is important to remember that a person's comfort with novelty or difference isn't merely a personal trait. Uncertainty avoidance is a worldview dimension that is culturally influenced and measures "the extent to which a society, organization, or group relies on social norms, rules, and procedures to alleviate the unpredictability of future events" (House et al., 2004, p. 30). Businesses that rely on tourism must take into account this worldview dimension because risk is a key concern for international travelers. Sojourners with a strong desire to avoid uncertainty tend to avoid unfamiliar experiences and look instead for symbols and structures that make sense to them (Hofstede, 1983; Yavas, 1990).

Cultures that avoid uncertainty embrace strict behavior rules that are taught and reinforced within the culture and view the world as full of truth and clarity. They negatively sanction ideas or behaviors that stray from the accepted norm. Cultures with higher tolerance for uncertainty maintain a more relaxed attitude and feel comfortable in unstructured situations. They are relaxed in situations where the rules for behavior are unclear. Different cultural systems tolerate different degrees of comfort when faced with ambiguity, what cannot be known, or what is outside of one's control (Hofstede, 1983).

Tourist Purchases and Uncertainty

Consumption characteristics of societies that have differing uncertainty tolerances also vary. In shopping, there are five types of risk that must be navigated:

1 financial (spending too much money)
2 functional (does not meet the need or work as assumed or promised)
3 physical (personal illness or injury as a consequence of misunderstanding cultural cues)
4 social (unfashionable or of poor quality)
5 psychological (damages self-esteem or causes guilt)

Of Hofstede's five cultural dimensions, uncertainty avoidance is considered the most influential ideological frame related to travel shopping. Tourists who seek to avoid uncertainty interact formally, keep meticulous records, and look for formal policies, clear justifications, and clear calculable values. They are particularly interested in tradition and authenticity in their purchasing and formalized statements to validate such claims. When shopping, they need to understand the market rules for pricing and the process of purchasing, step-by-step, before they enter a conversation about buying a product. Communicators seeking to avoid uncertainty do not like to spend much time on the process of purchasing. They are often highly emotional about purchasing or negotiating for goods, feel comfortable communicating emotions, and enjoy debating and negotiating.

Tourists from cultures that more comfortably tolerate uncertainty often interact informally and are less concerned about rules or errors. They embrace risks because they understand that value isn't necessarily fixed, and as such they are often unemotional about purchases or the negotiation processes surrounding them. In terms of communication, they are flexible and agreeable and adapt their behavior to others in the interaction. Their flexibility doesn't mean that they aren't invested in the outcome, but instead will meet their counterparts equally in a negotiation and will comfortably end the process if they feel disrespected or if little progress is made.

Cultural Contexts: Morocco and Norway

The first national culture in this case is Morocco. Morocco has little tolerance for uncertainty, ranking 68 on a 100-point scale. What this means is that, in general, Moroccan systems have a need for rigid codes of belief, security, and precision, and expect that cultural codes will be known and followed consistently. In their day-to-day interactions, Moroccans expect traditions to be respected, especially in terms of interaction norms. One simple example is greeting. There is a formula of welcome and salutation that is followed based on the relationship of the communicators and the context that all Moroccans respect and follow with minimal, if no, deviation. Similarly, in business contexts, there will be clear processes for negotiating contracts or opening accounts that will require all specific steps and people be accommodated in the correct order. (This is not to say that those steps will be articulated verbally, as the internalization versus externalization of information is found under the cultural dimension of context orientation.)

The second national culture in this case is Norway. Norway sits in the center of the uncertainty avoidance measure, at 50. This means that Norwegians are comfortable and adaptable with some ambiguity and are willing to take some risk and embrace innovation as long as interaction efforts are met equally and with minimal emotion. Norwegians, while respecting tradition, will adjust and amend processes and procedures to accommodate time factors, financial variables, or even personality differences. They like to know what will be happening, and as such embrace routines and schedules. Business meetings often have clear agendas, creative problem solving is embraced, and the few rules that are most important are followed.

Retail Aesthetics in Morocco

Many cultures have cottage industries for traditional artifacts that are designed to appeal to international tourists. Leather production, which has a long history in Fez, Morocco, and the preservation of the historic tanneries in the United Nations Educational, Scientific and Cultural Organization (UNESCO) World Heritage site of the Fez Medina are a focal point of the tourist experience in Morocco. Around nearly every corner in the Fez Medina is an opportunity to purchase wares of leather, crafted nearby in the famous leather souk. From key chains to handbags to Moroccan poufs (ottomans), a tourist can find traditional Moroccan-style leather products at various price points. Each little shop or booth (see Figure 8.1) contains similar items, and as shoppers wander through the mazes of the ancient city, they are invited to browse inside the stores with the traditional and formal greeting of the shopkeeper, "Welcome to you! Please, come in and look around!"

The small booths are designed to underscore the shopkeeper as the guardian of the products, and a formal shopping exchange where the best goods are presented formally and ceremonially, with long explanations to the potential buyer. Products are hung or laid out in such a way that do not invite random touch or window shopping from a distance, and prices are rarely displayed.

In the Moroccan shopping experience, bargaining is expected. Turn-taking for the purchase is highly ritualized, and there are rules of right and wrong. In many ways, it is a game, and as members of a culture with lower tolerance for uncertainty, it is an ideal form of communication with clear

FIGURE 8.1 A shop in Fez Medina, Morocco

Photo credit: Lizavetta/Shutterstock.com.

110 Mara K. Berkland

rules. In bargaining, two people or parties try to reach a joint agreement about the value of a good. The offering party spends a lot of time explaining the value points of the product of interest, citing its authenticity, its quality, its ties to tradition, and bits of emotional information about the relationship of the seller to the product or the burgeoning relationship/friendship between the negotiators. The potential buyer is expected to engage in the ritual, show the appropriate formality, show respect and warmth, and only engage in a purchasing conversation if there is true interest in the product because the bargaining process is expected to conclude with an agreement. In traditional bargaining exchanges, both interactants would be aware of the ideal price range for any product, so the monetary, social, and functional risks are minimal.

Retail Aesthetics in Norway

While visiting the Finmark region of Norway, tourists will learn extensively about the Sami people, the indigenous culture of the Norwegian Arctic, and their lifestyle and history. Surrounded by reindeer and learning about the herding traditions of the Sami, the tourist has the opportunity to see and purchase Sami art and jewelry. Silver jewelry is a popular tourist product that is highly prized for its quality and long history. A number of artisans sell jewelry in the traditional Sami style, and they are found in individual stores that are full of light and space, allowing for quiet browsing and solitary

FIGURE 8.2 Details of Juhl's Silver Gallery, Kautokeino, Norway

Photo credit: Juhl's Silver Gallery.

observation. One such store is Juhl's Silver Gallery in Kautokeino, Norway (see Figure 8.2).

Here, the potential buyer enters the showroom and is given a brief explanation of the history of both the Sami people's jewelry traditions and the Juhl family as artists and preservationists of the silversmithing tradition. After that, the patron is invited to wander at leisure, touching and looking as desired, and is asked only to seek assistance if wanting to try something on. Prices are clearly marked, and exchanges are direct with little socializing, emotional connection, or conversation. Customers are encouraged to ask questions, and the staff customizes their answers to each of the persons asking.

Uncertainty Avoidance in Retail Aesthetics

Shopping norms and the presentation of products can vary greatly. By comparing examples of the marketing and presentation of goods in two different national cultures, it is possible to see the impact of the dimension of uncertainty avoidance on the expected product consumption norms.

Presentation of Goods

One of the first things to note is the display and arrangement of the goods for purchase. Visual complexity influences uncertainty in important ways. The Moroccan market store is small and filled with goods. The leather wares cover the walls and displays, organized clearly by type. One should assume that the entire inventory is showcased for the shopper, and the layout is free form, without aisles or rows to arrange goods by type. The handbags and the poufs and the belts are all in the same space, and in many Moroccan stores, they are grouped interspersed with each other. The Norwegian store uses an aisle layout, and the jewelry and other goods are spaced and arranged on decorative elements to showcase their uniqueness and beauty.

Stores with low spatial complexity arrange displays and merchandise in rows and columns like the Norwegian example. Stores with high complexity display merchandise irregularly like the Moroccan example. Experienced tourists may prefer higher complexity in a store's arrangement of goods in part because the amount of information in a low-complexity arrangement is less. Shoppers from cultures that have low tolerance for uncertainty would find the sparse Norwegian display as potentially insufficient. Moroccan shoppers would need to see every purchase option and compare the qualities and characteristics in order to feel a reduced risk. In contrast, a consumer with higher tolerance for risk would not view the curated selection of goods as a potential problem, as those shoppers do not see the purchase experience as having a correct outcome, especially since they do not see values as fixed. Not seeing every potential purchase item would not make them feel as if they did not have enough information to make a safe purchase.

Pricing

The Norwegian silver store has clearly listed prices marked on both signs and price tags. The lack of such price tags in the Moroccan store necessitates the initiation of a bargaining process that requires back-and-forth interaction between the seller and the purchaser, where offers and information are exchanged.

Clearly stating pricing on a price tag or a sign, rather than bargaining, is normative for cultures with higher tolerance for uncertainty. Those who tolerate ambiguity and risk are unemotional about their purchases and are less concerned about having an impact on the price because they see value as subjective. Cultures with low tolerance for uncertainty have greater instances of bargaining behavior and are greatly interested in the outcome of the exchange to mitigate financial risk, having paid more than necessary, and social and psychological risks, such as looking foolish or feeling self-doubt by having been swindled into paying more.

The shopper who tolerates ambiguity will embrace the idea of fixed pricing. The reason that fixed pricing is appealing to someone with less risk aversion is because it gives the shopper the opportunity to assess whether they agree with suggested value, rather, if what the shopper sees as their subjective value is in line with the suggested value. The shopper seeking to avoid uncertainty will struggle with the fixed price strategy as there is no way for them to get to or assess a true price, which should emerge in the exchange between the seller and the buyer.

Bargaining, however, is more comfortable for the shopper looking to reduce risk because face-to-face encounters with salespeople are considered a key variable to reduce financial risk and uncertainty. The uncertainty avoiding shoppers will enter the store and offer a first bid on an item that is modest, in that they will offer a price that they think is right. The ensuing negotiation will demonstrate emotion, because the display of emotions helps communicators make rapid judgments about context clues by quickly guiding appropriate behavior. Because the negotiation will be one of degrees, the risk-avoidant shoppers will not adapt to the seller's behavior, and requests for large price adjustments will not be met. In general, the interaction will take place, whether successful or not, relatively quickly.

Comparatively, the uncertainty tolerant negotiators are more relaxed and will change their behaviors to mirror those of the seller. For them, the interaction is an attempt to figure out what they, personally, are willing to pay for the article. They do not show their emotions and are unsettled if the sellers do, as they see this as merely a subjective exchange with no right answer, requiring more interaction and time than necessary to conclude. While they will end the bargaining if little progress is made, they are more adaptable and give more in the interaction, though they would prefer to make a decision without the exchange (Hofstede, Jonker, & Verwaart, 2008).

Product Education

Souvenir purchasing is a way to touch and keep the authentic experience of cultural tourism. Purchasing a souvenir that is inauthentic is risky. There is a social risk to the buyer in that the purchase of an inauthentic or poorly made item could make the tourist look foolish and uneducated. There is also a psychological risk to purchasing souvenirs if one's self-esteem is tied to being able to recognize authentic or valuable cultural symbols. People from highly risk avoidant cultures tend to seek certainty by looking for certification via formal rules and regulations and heeding the advice of accepted experts.

Three key components of the Moroccan shopping experience communicate authenticity to the potential buyer. First, the location of the leather goods stores in the medina and often within the leather souk itself, next to the historic, still functioning tanneries serves as a direct message of authenticity. Being able to prove that a cultural souvenir is locally handmade reduces the risk of the object being inauthentic. In the case of the Moroccan leather goods, the consumer can see the vats of chemicals and the drying animal skins and smell the curing leather as the scent fills the air. Similarly, when purchasing such items in the medina, the shopper will see the same products being worn by the locals, especially the babouche (leather shoes) and bags, increasing the sense that they are truly of the region. Second, the accessibility of the Moroccan goods in the store allows the consumer to touch them, compare them, and scrutinize them for cheap or low-quality indicators that would reveal an inexpert artisan. As tourists are invited to open, try on, examine, bend, and even pour water on the leather goods, which lowers the risk of choosing a leather product of poor quality. Third, through the bargaining process, the communication about the authenticity or quality of the product is at the forefront. Often, the first turn of the Moroccan salesperson, before stating a price, will be to walk the potential buyer through the features of the souvenir as well as the production of leather goods in general. The seller sees it as their job to talk specifically about the souvenirs in terms of their origin, their uniqueness, and the materials and processes used to make them. Great care will also be taken to point out cultural symbols and to explain their meaning. In particular, in Fez, there will be a strong emphasis on clarifying which goods were made in Fez and which ones might have been made elsewhere in Morocco.

The Norwegian silver stores also work to educate the consumer, but with less details about the specific design or souvenir being considered by the buyer. As one enters the store, the shopper will be educated, via a series of signs or placards and by a brief explanation, about the Sami people, the local artist producing the jewelry, and the region. These explanations help to reassure the buyer that the goods in the store are of a historic tradition, often by an artist who is of the local indigenous Sami culture or who has studied the tradition. An explanation of the connection to the traditional culture for each item or design is not explained, however, and while a shopper might be able to inquire and get an answer, the general educational materials are expected to sufficiently dispel any concerns about a lack of authenticity.

Negotiating Differences in Shopping Concerns

Morocco and Norway vary enough, at 68 and 50, respectively, in their comfort levels with uncertainty to demonstrate differences in preferred retail store design and customer interaction. The ability to tryout, taste, touch, compare, and access further information which can be assessed based on the nonverbals and emotions of the seller is key in the world of the highly risk-averse shopper. The shopper who embraces risk, rather than attempts to avoid it, will make decisions based on personal interest and desire, need fewer options for choice and less education about the product, and will desire unemotional interaction. In all, they will likely find the crowded stores, strong demand for interaction, and the lack of clear pricing confusing as those factors will impede personal, subjective decision-making about what they see as the worth of an item. In a sense, there are too many stimuli to consider. Shoppers with high risk aversion need significantly more stimuli to be able to assess, not their personal desire or interest in a product, but how that souvenir compares to other potential options, the level of authenticity that they can assess based on provided information, and the personal, formal interactions with sellers that allow them to understand and effect the financial risk.

Tolerance for uncertainty is just one of the dimensions that can explain how shoppers go about selecting goods or how retailers set up the buying experience for consumers. The retail aesthetics described here clearly show how that dimension is embedded differently in different cultural contexts. Reducing uncertainty means reducing risk, whether the risk be financial, functional, physical, social, or psychological. Of Hofstede's five cultural dimensions, uncertainty avoidance is considered the most influential ideological frame related to travel shopping because tourists are already disequilibrated by being outside of their home cultures.

Discussion Questions

- How does the layout of the products and how customers are expected to interact in each shopping experience differ?
- What are the risks of buying something while traveling?
- How is authenticity presented in each circumstance? Where does the information come from and why is that important?
- How might the display of emotions make shopping seem less risky?
- How does being a cultural outsider create risk and uncertainty?

Suggestions for Further Reading

Cohen, E. (1972). Toward a sociology of international tourism. *Social Research, 39*, 164–182. https://www.jstor.org/stable/40970087

Hume, D. (2013). *Tourism art and souvenirs: The material culture of tourism*. Milton Park: Routledge.

Koc, E. (2020). *Cross-cultural aspects of tourism and hospitality: A services marketing and management perspective*. Milton Park: Routledge.

Singh, S., Timothy, D. J., & Dowling, R. K. (Eds.). (2003). *Tourism in destination communities*. Wallingford: CABI.

Timothy, D. J. (2005). *Shopping tourism, retailing and leisure*. Clevedon: Channel View Publications.

References

Hofstede, G. (1983). National cultures in four dimensions: A research-based theory of cultural differences among nations. *International Studies of Management & Organization, 13*(1–2), 46–74. https://doi.org/10.1080/00208825.1983.11656358

Hofstede, G. J., Jonker, C. M., & Verwaart, T. (2008, December). An agent model for the influence of culture on bargaining. In *Proceedings of the 1st International Working Conference on Human Factors and Computational Models in Negotiation* (pp. 39–46). New York: Association for Computing Machinery. http://mmi.tudelft.nl/~catholijn/cve/Prelim_versions/hucom2008Culture.pdf

House, R. J., Hanges, P. J., Javidan, M., Dorfman, P. W., & Gupta, V. (Eds.). (2004). *Culture, leadership, and organizations: The GLOBE study of 62 societies*. Thousand Oaks, CA: Sage Publications.

Law, R., & Au, N. (2000). Relationship modeling in tourism shopping: a decision rules induction approach. *Tourism Management, 21*(3), 241–249. https://doi.org/10.1016/S0261-5177(99)00056-4

Murphy, L., Moscardo, G., Benckendorff, P., & Pearce, P. (2011). Evaluating tourist satisfaction with the retail experience in a typical tourist shopping village.

Journal of retailing and Consumer Services, 18(4), 302–310. https://doi.org/10.21832/9781873150610

Yavas, U. (1990). Correlates of vacation travel: Some empirical evidence. *Journal of Professional Services Marketing, 5*(2), 3–18. https://doi.org/10.1300/J090v05n02_02

Yuksel, A. (2004). Shopping experience evaluation: A case of domestic and international visitors. *Tourism Management, 25*(6), 751–759.

9
CULTURAL COMPARISON OF CURRENCY DEMAND IN ARGENTINA AND INDIA

Brenden J. Mason and Kabir Dasgupta

When an economic exchange takes place, the transaction generates an increase in income for one party and an increase in expenditure for the other. For the economy as a whole, the total amount of income should, in principle, equal the total amount of expenditure, which, in turn, should equal the total amount of final goods and services produced in a country in a given time period. At the national level, income—and therefore expenditure—is measured as gross domestic product, more popularly known by its initials, GDP. A country's GDP equals the sum of expenditures on final goods by consumers, firms, government, and foreigners.

There are income-generating economic exchanges that are *not* recorded in the official GDP statistics, however. For instance, if someone cuts hair out of a garage for friends in exchange for a few bucks, such transactions will not have a direct impact on GDP; they go undetected. Of course, there are many other unrecorded transactions that are more nefarious or illegal in nature. The sum of such transactions constitutes what economists call the "informal sector," also known as the "shadow economy."

In the shadow economy, the medium of economic exchange is currency, that is, cash and coins. If someone goes to a neighbor's garage for a haircut and pays with cash, nobody knows about the transaction except the buyer and the seller. The buyer doesn't have to worry whether the payment will clear their bank. The seller doesn't have to deal with state inspections. And neither party pays a sales tax. If a country has a thriving shadow economy, the demand for currency will likely be quite high, and this demand spills over into the formal economy.

This chapter examines currency demand, appealing to the cases of Argentina and India. India's cash demand has been recently trending upward because of a pervasive underground economy. Argentina's is on a downward trend due to an uncontained rate of inflation.

Inflation

Inflation is the phenomenon where the prices of goods and services in an economy increase. As prices increase, consumers require more currency to make the same number of transactions. Hence, as prices increase, currency demand increases.

It is easy to see the lost value of currency because of inflation if we examine savings. In addition to using currency to make purchases, sometimes people store their cash as a form of savings. The benefit of saving money in the form of cash is that it's immediately available in the case of an unexpected expense or an emergency. In that case, the savings can be drawn upon quickly. But this benefit comes with a cost: inflation reduces the purchasing power of those savings. The same amount of cash will buy fewer and fewer goods and services.

Banks

Banks can mitigate the erosion that inflation has on savings by paying interest on deposits. As inflation cuts into the value of currency, people may be tempted to withdraw their savings. To prevent this, banks generally pay more interest when inflation is higher. With deposits intact, banks can fund more loans and provide other services.

One service that banks offer is the physical protection of deposits. Holding savings in the form of cash is risky in that it can be lost, stolen, or destroyed. Banks alleviate this problem by keeping funds safe. Most banks have vaults and security guards to protect the deposits. Furthermore, in many countries, deposits are insured, often by the government.

Banks also allow quick access to cash should a person need it. Most banks have branches, automated teller machines (ATMs), paper checks, and debit cards. Debit cards aren't cash, of course, but they function in much the same way: one swipe, insertion, or tap of the card, and within seconds the funds are transferred from the buyer's account to the seller's account. This immediate transfer of funds happens with income payments as well: direct deposit is a common service offered by banks and employers.

But workers in the shadow economy would likely not want direct deposit. They may fear that the government will be able to see their income and perhaps tax them accordingly. Shadow market consumers, too, might not want to make purchases using checks or a debit card because it leaves a paper trail. The bank employees, and possibly others, can see which purchases were made, to whom, and when.

Banks sometimes offer credit cards. Like cash and debit cards, credit cards can be used to make purchases. And like cash and savings accounts, credit cards can also absorb unexpected shocks to income or expenditures. For instance, people may put away a fraction of their income to save for an emergency or "a rainy day." But with a credit card, such precautionary saving is no longer necessary. If an unanticipated expenditure should arise, it can be covered with the credit card. The consumer pays the debt back over time, likely in installments. The overall, final payment is greater, but the benefit is that the expenditure is spread out across time. Credit cards, therefore, allow saved income to earn interest by keeping the savings in savings account or perhaps another financial asset.

Cultural Dimension: Uncertainty Avoidance

According to the popular Hofstede framework of cross-cultural studies, culture is "among other things, a set of likely reactions of citizens with a common mental programming" (Hofstede, Hofstede, & Minkov, 2010, p. 191). One aspect of culture that is acutely relevant for monetary economics is the degree to which a society abhors ambiguity, also known as "uncertainty avoidance." Hofstede, Hofstede, and Minkov (2010, p. 191) define uncertainty avoidance as *"the extent to which the members of a culture feel threatened by ambiguous or unknown situations."* [Emphasis theirs.] Thus, in cultures that avoid uncertainty, there may be an acceptance of familiar risks, but a "fear of ambiguous situations and of unfamiliar risks" (Hofstede, Hofstede, & Minkov, 2010, p. 203).

Some unfamiliar risks can be managed by holding cash. For example, if someone's income becomes unstable, they can hold more money to smooth the fluctuations. People who are skeptical of digital payment technologies can hold more cash. People who fear going into credit card debt or are weary of keeping funds in a bank can hold cash instead. Cash is countable and tangible, which brings with it a kind of peace of mind. Someone fearful of not having funds available for an emergency can hold money as a kind of precaution. Additionally, if someone doesn't want to put their savings into stocks or bonds because the returns are too volatile, they can hold money instead.

Nevertheless, holding currency comes with its own risks. Cash can be lost, stolen, or destroyed. Dealing in cash risks exchanging or receiving counterfeit bills, which are worthless. Additionally, storing wealth in the form of cash brings with it the risk of its value being eroded by inflation.

Cultural Contexts: Argentina and India

To understand how economies balance such opposing forces, we focus on two countries: Argentina and India. There are four major factors that affect the amount of currency in circulation: income, prices, banks, and uncertainty. These factors influence cash holdings in opposite ways: income and prices (to a point) are positively related to the demand for currency, while bankcards and interest rates are negatively related. The degree of uncertainty avoidance has an ambiguous relationship to cash demand; it depends on how "uncertainty" or "risk" is defined.

India scores 40 on the uncertainty dimension and has a more centrist preference for avoiding uncertainty. India accepts imperfection, is patient, and tolerates the unexpected. The concept of adjusting is one that sits front and center, and while people comfortably settle into routines, rules are not set and stone and are frequently bypassed.

By comparison, Argentina scores very high on uncertainty dimension, at 86. This positioning is reflected in a strong need for rules and a legal system to both enforce them and create additional rules to clarify them, or sometimes adjust them to serve the powerful. Despite the existence of rules, corruption is high and average individuals don't always obey the laws, creating a shadow system of interaction outside of the formal structure (Hofstede Insights, 2022).

Despite this extreme difference, one area in which India and Argentina are similar is their use of cash. Cash usage is widespread in each country. The year 2016 perfectly exemplifies the important role of cash in the respective economies. In that year, both Argentina and India introduced new currency denominations, which is an unusual occurrence in modern times. This would be akin to the United States adding a $200 banknote to its portfolio of bill denominations or in Japan introducing a 25,000-yen note. Argentina issued new notes because inflation had been eroding the value of those already in circulation. India, meanwhile, removed two denominations from circulation and replaced them with alternatives to strike a blow to the nation's shadow economy.

Currency Demand Comparison

Figure 9.1 is a dual-axis chart depicting economic data from Argentina on the top (Panel A) and India on the bottom (Panel B). The data come from the Bank for International Settlements (BIS).

A dual-axis chart is helpful and often used in economics to show two series of different magnitudes. A dual axis facilitates seeing the co-movement in the two series. On the left axis of Figure 9.1 is the fraction of income

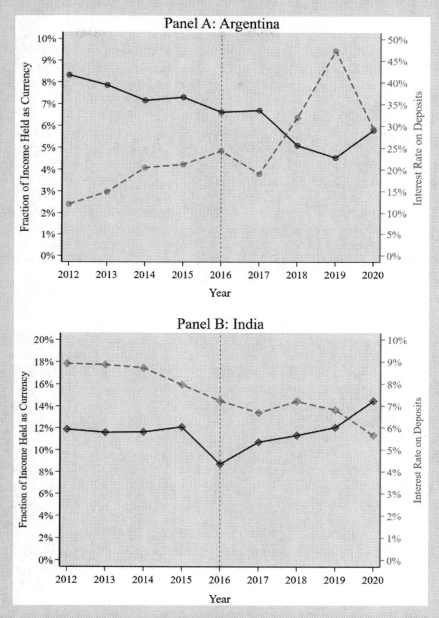

FIGURE 9.1 Currency as a fraction of GDP and interest rate on savings deposits

held as currency (dark solid line). Total currency in circulation (CIC) is divided by total national income (denominated in the local currency—pesos for Argentina and rupees for India). "Income" is defined as nominal GDP, where "nominal" simply means that it hasn't been adjusted for inflation. The right axis plots the interest rate on bank deposits. These data come from the respective governments (central banks). The horizontal axis is time, measured in years.

Focusing on the left axis, the dark solid line yields some insights, independent of looking at the axis on the right. When the solid is decreasing, that means that the numerator, CIC, is decreasing faster than the denominator—and vice versa. For example, in Argentina, the fraction of income held in currency has, for most years, fallen; it's a long, downward trend. This means that Argentina's income, which, again, is not adjusted for inflation, has grown faster than currency holdings, which results in a falling fraction. In India, the situation is reversed: other than the dip in 2016 (explained below), there is a gradual increase in the demand for currency relative to income. It is also noteworthy to compare the magnitudes: India's CIC/GDP ratio is notably higher than Argentina's, demonstrating that national currency is relatively more prevalent in the Indian economy.

The right axis (light dashed line) for each panel corresponds to the interest rate on bank deposits. Once again, the respective patterns of Argentina and India are trending in opposite directions. Argentina's rate steadily increases over time, while India's is steadily decreasing. The magnitudes of the interest rate in the two countries are also noteworthy. India's range of 5%–9% is relatively high by global standards, but small compared to Argentina's range of 12%–45%.

The vertical dashed line for 2016 crosses both panels because a rare economic phenomenon happened this year: in both countries, the government introduced new currency notes. However, the rationale was completely different: Argentina because of rampant inflation and India because of its robust shadow economy.

Figure 9.2 contains data from the World Bank on Argentina (ARD) and India (IND) regarding close substitutes for currency, both in its role as a medium of exchange (for spending) and in its role as a store of value (for saving). The data are country averages from a triennial survey across the years 2011, 2014, 2017, and 2021.

In Argentina, approximately 43% of people own a debit card, while 25% own a credit card. In India, the rates are much lower for both: 22% own a debit card and about 3% own a credit card. By comparison, in the United States, these figures are much higher: about 80% ownership for debit cards, 66% for credit cards.

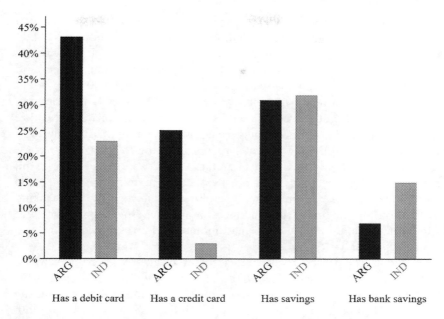

FIGURE 9.2 Close substitutes for currency: Argentina (ARG) and India (IND)

Almost one-third of both Argentinians and Indians have saved at least some amount of their earnings, but the number of people with savings *in a bank account,* a possible substitute for cash, drops off markedly for both countries, especially Argentina. As a reference, within the same survey, about 80% of U.S. respondents have savings, and about 60% have savings in a bank account.

India's Shadow Economy and Demonetization

Figure 9.1B clearly illustrates that cash is crucial in India. India is cash-centric because of its vast shadow economy, which is estimated to employ 80% of the total workforce (Lahiri, 2020). Some of the common jobs in the Indian shadow economy include construction workers, small farmers, domestic help, beedi rolling, and leather working. In urban areas, many informal laborers work roadside, selling various goods and services such as fast food, clothing, shoe-shining, and massages. These workers deal exclusively in cash and, by doing so, evade taxes.

The sizable shadow economy hasn't gone unnoticed by government officials. In November 2016, the Indian government unexpectedly announced a plan to strike at the heart of the shadow economy: remove from circulation the two highest banknotes, the 500-rupee note (INR500) and the

1,000-rupee note (INR1,000), together accounting for 87% of the total value of currency holdings. This demonetization plan did not merely pull these denominations from circulation; they were rendered immediately *illegal* to use in transactions. Between the November announcement and December 31, 2016, anyone who had INR500 or INR1,000 notes could redeem them for a newly designed INR500 or a completely new denomination, the INR2,000. People could either exchange their about-to-be-defunct currency for the new notes or deposit their demonetized bills into bank accounts. But there was a catch: people wanting to swap old notes for new ones faced a 4,000-rupee daily limit. People wanting to deposit old notes into a bank account faced no such limit. The hope was that people would open a bank account. The government could then use the banking system to shine a light on the shadow economy: deposits in a bank account can be easily monitored for abnormal amounts and investigated for tax evasion (Lahiri, 2020).

Naturally, the process of note replacement led to a "cash crunch" in the Indian economy, which resulted in production disruptions. In Figure 9.1B, an economy-wide decrease in output would lower income, increasing the CIC/GDP ratio. After 2016, Panel B does indeed show an upward trend, consistent with research on the effects of demonetization. For example, areas that experienced the cash shortage more intensely saw greater declines in economic activity (Chodorow-Reich et al., 2020). Cash-reliant firms purchased fewer raw materials and hired fewer workers (Subramaniam, 2020). The average time lost by waiting at the bank to exchange old notes for new ones was around seven hours—a full workday. Rather than waiting in line, many villagers paid a premium to local moneylenders to exchange their soon-to-be-illegal currency (Zhu et al., 2018). The Indian monetary authority responded to such disruptions by cutting interest rates (Figure 9.1B) to stimulate spending, which had fallen because of the demonetization.

Was the demonetization policy a success? On the one hand, yes: Figure 9.1B shows a pronounced dip in currency in circulation in 2016—a direct result of the demonetization. On the other hand, no: aside from the output and labor market disruptions mentioned above, Figure 9.2 shows that cards and bank savings are still mostly unpopular in India, even when examining the latest data from 2021. And after 2016, the currency-to-income ratio reverts to its pre-2016 trend. Cash is still a dominant force in the Indian economy.

Argentina's Inflation and New Currency Notes

As a contrast to India, Argentina has seen a long *downward* trend in currency holdings relative to national income, as shown in Figure 9.1A. Income in

Argentina has been increasing. This sounds like a good thing, but it is *prices* rather than *quantities* that have been increasing. Hence, Argentina's decline in the CIC/GDP ratio is primarily the result of inflation, not an increase in material well-being. At one point, the inflation rate was so high throughout this period, that the government fudged the inflation numbers, prompting private economists to develop their own estimates (Cavallo & Rigobon, 2016).

As prices increase rapidly, each currency note buys fewer and fewer goods and services. Prior to 2016, the highest bill denomination of the Argentine peso (ARS) was ARS100, which, in 2012, was able to purchase about $22 worth of goods and services in the United States. Inflation was so out of control that just four years later, in 2016, that same 100-peso bill would have purchased just $6.78 worth of U.S. goods and services.

With the value of each bill in circulation rapidly falling, the government introduced two new currency notes: ARS200 ($13.54) and ARS500 ($33.85). This was not a measure to try to combat inflation (if anything, this would have further stoked inflation). Instead, this was a policy to try to meet the needs of consumers and their personal spending habits. Alas, this would not be enough. While the ARS200 and ARS500 began circulating, inflation was still running hot. In 2017, the government introduced yet another, even higher denomination: ARS1000, which, at the time, had a U.S. dollar value of $60.41, but, as of the end of 2020, had a value of $14.21, again reiterating that inflation has been high and persistent throughout the decade. As can be seen in Figure 9.1A, the currency in circulation increased relative to GDP from 2016 to 2017, likely as a direct result of the introduction of the new bills.

To compensate bank account holders for the loss of value to the Argentine peso, the government raised the interest rates. This explains the upward trend in interest rates, which is especially sharp from 2017 to 2018. One of the hopes of the increase was that people would save money rather than spend it, for it is the *spending*—consumer spending in particular—of currency that ultimately drives inflation. Not coincidentally, 2018 also witnessed a relatively steep fall in currency in the currency-to-income ratio (Figure 9.1A), in part, because the opportunity cost of holding cash was so high. In other words, holding cash became expensive in terms of foregone interest payments.

Banks and Credit

Figure 9.2 indicates that Indians save money, but not with banks; cards aren't popular either. The lack of take-up can be explained by the difficulty in accessing banks: approximately two-thirds of India's population is rural. Distance to a bank reduces the opportunity cost of holding cash. Suppose there's a financial emergency in a rural location. A villager would prefer keeping cash in the home rather than making a long trip to the bank because of the substantial costs in terms of time and effort. Such costs are apparently so great that rural Indians aren't persuaded to save using a bank account despite earning a return of 6%–9% (Figure 9.1B).

In response to the substantial number of unbanked Indians, the newly elected government in 2014 enacted a major initiative to promote financial services in underbanked areas of the country, the *Pradhan Mantri Jan Dhan Yojana*. The program facilitated effortless access to bank services like direct deposit. A salient feature of the program is that it allows people to open bank accounts even with a zero balance. The government eagerly promoted the program, going door to door, thereby making it easy to open an account.

Initially, the program seemed successful: many Indians opened a bank account. Nonetheless, Figure 9.2 shows that despite the increase in new accounts, Indians aren't using them: the number of Indians with a debit card from 2017 to 2021 has actually *fallen;* 48% of Indian adults have an inactive account, the highest in the world. What went wrong? Cash is too ingrained in the Indian economy, probably because of the ever-present shadow economy. Research has shown that debit and credit cards will not be adopted until the shadow economy is reduced (Marmora & Mason, 2021).

Like Indians, approximately 30% of Argentines have saved at least some of their income over the past 12 months (Figure 9.2). However, less than 10% have saved using a bank account despite an abnormally high interest rate on savings deposits (Figure 9.1A). The leading explanation for Argentina's hesitancy to rely on banks and credit products is the country's history with banks and, specifically, the government oversight of these institutions. In 2001, Argentina's economy saw what can only be described as the world's twenty-first century equivalent of the Great Depression. GDP fell dramatically; unemployment abounded. Despite deposits being federally insured, there was a bank run, that is, people—quite literally—ran to their banks to withdraw funds. As a response, the Argentine government, in an attempt to stabilize the banking system, limited the amount of withdrawals to ARS1,000 per month. This limit on deposits—also known as the *corralito*—caused riots and looting.

For those Argentines who mistrust banks, the alternative is often hoarding cash, but not the Argentine peso. Instead, many Argentines hoard U.S. dollars, which is something that they have been doing since their previous bouts with extremely high inflation (Perry & Servén, 2003). In fact, the practice is so widespread that the government cracks down on it, limiting the amount of U.S. dollars that Argentines can legally purchase per month.

An entire industry has developed in Argentina's shadow economy exchanging Argentine pesos for U.S. dollars. The exchangers are called *arbolitos*. The hoarding of U.S. dollars partly explains why, despite an interest rate of 40% (Figure 9.1A), Argentine demand for currency is still high by world standards.

Cultural Considerations

On the Hofstede uncertainty avoidance index, Argentina is an 86 out of a 100-point scale, while India is a 40. Based on these cultural dimension scores and given that cash is a way to mitigate some economic risks, we might expect Argentina to hold more cash than India. But Figure 9.1 shows this not to be the case (perhaps unless we included foreign currency holdings). Savings also help buffer adverse income shocks, for example, an unexpected car repair. But Figure 9.2 shows that the two countries have approximately the same rate of savings. The upshot is that while uncertainty avoidance plays a role in a nation's demand for currency, there are other factors that counteract the desire to hold cash as a kind of insurance against risk: economic elements such as the shadow economy, inflation, and ubiquity of banking services, and cultural considerations such as family ties, religion, and trust-mistrust.

Cash is an integral part of the Indian culture. In India, currency functions beyond market-based transactions of goods and services. Currency bears significance in human relationships as well as in religious practices. For instance, cash gifts, popularly known as *shagun* in the northern part of India, are often used as a medium to express kinship love and affection for younger family members during celebrations of festivals and major life events such as wedding ceremonies or birthdays. Furthermore, making cash-based donations at religious institutions is also a part of the Indian tradition of honoring one's unreserved faith in God. This is an age-old practice that is unanimously followed by most believers regardless of their economic condition. The significance of such contributions in the Indian culture is evident from the fact that some Hindu temples receive donations worth more than US $80 million every year.[1] These donations are made mainly in the form of cash (or possibly gold from the super wealthy).

Argentina has an entrenched distrust of banks. It wasn't just 2001 that caused the skepticism. Argentines also remember the inflation from the 1980s and the ensuing bank run of 1989. Even as recently as 2019 there was a bank run at just the hint of some political instability. From a culture standpoint, trust falls under uncertainty avoidance (Minkov & Hofstede, 2014). In cultures that avoid uncertainty, they may be generally distrustful of others. Some scholars explicitly measure a distrust-trust dimension

(Beugelsdijk & Welzel, 2018). Along with several other Latin American countries that have had severe bouts of inflation, Argentina scores relatively low on trust. Argentines save in the form of cash, but it's typically not their own currency; it's U.S. dollars, which minimizes the risk of its value being eroded by inflation and the risk of its access being restricted by the bank or the government.

Conclusion

Income, prices, interest rates, and uncertainty play major roles in the demand for currency. Technology and credit also affect the demand for cash. As income increases, the demand for cash increases, especially income that is earned in the shadow economy. As prices increase, the demand for cash also increases, but only to a point: if prices increase in an uncontrollable fashion, consumers get rid of cash by spending it quickly or moving their savings into an alternative asset—possibly foreign cash, for example, U.S. dollars in much of Latin America. Argentina's economic history is filled with bouts of high inflation, including in recent times, which has bred mistrust. Inflation is so high that it makes holding cash costly, especially when interest rates are astronomical. India's shadow economy is possibly the largest on earth, the lifeblood of which is cash. What's more, cash is embedded into other facets of Indian culture, such as religion and familial relationships.

These two countries share an infrequent economic phenomenon: the introduction of new banknotes. Despite the peso's rapidly falling value, the Argentine government issued new bills so that consumers could fund their purchases. India demonetized, taking high-denomination notes out of circulation and substituting them for new ones, all in an attempt to thwart the tax-evading effects of the shadow economy. Going forward, money will probably become more digital, which will likely require the use of banks. However, banks and credit card companies have had a difficult time penetrating these two economies, both of which are heavily dependent on paper currency.

Discussion Questions

- How might risk or uncertainty affect debit or credit card ownership?
- For both the buyer and the seller, are there any risks in using a debit or credit card to make economic transactions?
- How would very high inflation affect a positive credit card balance?
- Would more bank branches increase or decrease the currency in circulation?
- Could inflation affect the shadow economy? If so, how?
- In Figure 9.1, what does the steepness of the lines convey?

Note

1 The information pertains to the *Tirumala Tirupati Venkateswara* temple in the southern state of Andhra Pradesh is one of the richest temples in India (https://www.tourmyindia.com/blog/most-revered-and-rich-temples-of-india/).

Suggestions for Further Reading

Coyle, D. (2014). *GDP*. Princeton, NJ: Princeton University Press.
Patel, R., & Meaning, J. (2022). *Can't we just print more money?* London: Penguin Books.
Rogoff, K. S. (2016). *The curse of cash*. Princeton, NJ: Princeton University Press.
Wheelan, C. (2017). *Naked money*. New York: W.W. Norton & Company.

References

Beugelsdijk, S., & Welzel, C. (2018). Dimensions and dynamics of national culture: Synthesizing Hofstede with Inglehart. *Journal of Cross-Cultural Psychology, 49*(10), 1469–1505.
Cavallo, A., & Rigobon, R. (2016). The billion prices project: Using online prices for measurement and research. *Journal of Economic Perspectives, 30*(2), 151–178.
Chodorow-Reich, G., Gopinath, G., Mishra, P., & Narayanan, A. (2020). Cash and the economy: Evidence from India's demonetization. *The Quarterly Journal of Economics, 135*(1), 57–103.
Hofstede, G., Hofstede, G. J., & Minkov, M. (2010). *Cultures and organizations*. New York: McGraw-Hill.
Hofstede Insights. (2022). *National cultures: Culture comparison tool*. https://www.hofstede-insights.com/
Lahiri, A. (2020). The great Indian demonetization. *Journal of Economic Perspectives, 34*(1), 55–74.
Marmora, P., & Mason, B. J. (2021). Does the shadow economy mitigate the effect of cashless payment technology on currency demand? Dynamic panel evidence. *Applied Economics, 53*(6), 703–718.
Minkov, M., & Hofstede, G. (2014). A replication of Hofstede's uncertainty avoidance dimension across nationally representative samples from Europe. *International Journal of Cross-Cultural Management, 14*(2), 161–171.
Perry, G. E., & Servén, L. (2003). *The anatomy of a multiple crisis: Why was Argentina special and what can we learn from it?* SSRN 636443. https://ssrn.com/abstract=636443
Subramaniam, G. (2020). *The supply-side effects of India's demonetization*. SSRN 3472758. https://ssrn.com/abstract=3472758
Zhu, H., Gupta, A., Majumder, B., & Steinbach, S. (2018). Short-term effects of India's demonetization on the rural poor. *Economics Letters, 170*, 117–121.

10
CULTURAL INTERPRETATION OF INTERNATIONAL FINANCIAL REPORTING STANDARDS IN THE ANGLO-SAXON AND CONTINENTAL MODELS OF ACCOUNTING

Katarzyna Koleśnik and Sylwia Silska-Gembka

For many years, accounting has been serving humans in the development of civilization. Accounting, as an element of an information system, is a reliable source of various data for regulatory, social, economic, and environmental purposes. Every country in recent history has developed its own accounting system based on cultural values and priorities. The similarities and differences in national accounting systems between countries have led researchers to classify them into wider categories or models. Currently, two accounting systems are frequently used throughout the world: (1) the Anglo-Saxon model of accounting and (2) the continental model of accounting (also called the French-German model of accounting).

Toward International Financial Reporting Standards

The Anglo-Saxon model of accounting first appeared in the UK in the nineteenth century and arose as a consequence of the industrial revolution. It was mainly developed in countries where accounting was oriented toward the decision needs of large numbers of investors and creditors. In this model, the relationship of the business with the investors has a leading role in the economy, while the state does not hold much importance. The Anglo-Saxon model is strongly influenced by professional accounting bodies rather than government and relies upon terms such as "fair" and "true" or "presented fairly". As this model provides a more principles-based approach to financial reporting with less detailed guidance, interpreting and applying accounting rules requires accountants to apply professional, subjective judgment.

DOI: 10.4324/9781003298199-14

The continental model of accounting first appeared in France in the seventeenth century and was developed by Germany after its 1870 unification. It was mainly embraced and developed in countries where investors' interests were less important, due to the fact that capital market's role in providing finance was less important than banks which finance firms through loans. This model has a special appeal for countries in which the legal systems and the accounting rules are codified by government ministries. It serves for tax assessment and for the principle of conservatism based on historical cost and the use of depreciation. Conservatism is a perspective that understates gains and overstates losses to report lower net income and lower financial future benefits. Ultimately, this approach paints an austere picture of future growth, which can encourage caution in future financial decisions. Firms in continental European countries generally report more conservatively than firms in the Anglo-Saxon countries where attracting investors by showing potential growth is paramount (Hartmann, Marton, & Andersson Sols, 2020).

Consider, for example, the treatment of provisions. A company that expects to lose a lawsuit must recognize an economic loss (provision). That means that it must create a provision for expenditure which has not actually been committed to at the balance sheet date, and this will have the effect of reducing profits and (on the face of it) increasing liabilities. A consistently conservative firm will report such losses soon after the trial begins, while a less conservative one in similar situation will report such losses gradually as the trial process progresses.

Globalization of business and capital markets has created a need for a common global accounting system. Establishment of supranational enterprises has complicated international economic relations and revealed the need to standardize accounting regulations. A major step toward the standardization of accounting practices has been achieved by the adoption of International Financial Reporting Standards (IFRS) (since 2005) by all member states of the European Union (EU), plus many other countries such as Australia, New Zealand, Russia, and South Africa. The application of uniform accounting standards has reduced, but not automatically unified, all the solutions in accounting practices adopted by various countries. Despite national implementations of IFRS, significant differences between practice and IFRS still remain (Nobes, 2006; Wehrfritz & Haller, 2014).

Cultural Influence and Accounting

Accounting is shaped by the environment in which it operates. Just as nations have different histories, values, and political systems, they also have different patterns of financial accounting development (Mueller, Gernon, & Meek, 1994, p. 1). The cultural system has a powerful influence reflecting and influencing human behavior and social values, and its impact on accounting practices cannot be ignored. The fact that cultural values are embedded in accounting models means that attempts at standardization constitute attempts to impose one cultural viewpoint—an Anglo-Saxon one—on the entire world. This means discarding the ideology of other countries, specifically that represented in the continental model of accounting.

Cross-cultural research on the influence of culture on various accounting issues has almost exclusively relied on the cultural values set forth by Hofstede (Heidhues & Patel, 2011). Based on Hofstede's original model, Gray (1988) introduced cultural dimensions (power distance, uncertainty avoidance, individualism, masculinity) into accounting by creating four contrasting accounting values: (1) professionalism/statutory control, (2) uniformity/flexibility, (3) conservatism/optimism, and (4) secrecy/transparency. In his later work, Hofstede added fifth and sixth cultural dimensions: long- versus short-term orientation (also called "Confucian dynamism") and indulgence versus restraint (Hofstede, Hofstede, & Minkov, 2010), respectively. This chapter focuses on two of Gray's values: conservatism/optimism and secrecy/transparency, because conservatism and secrecy most strongly affect the valuation and level of disclosure in financial statements (see Table 10.1).

Conservatism and secrecy are regarded as a feature of accounting value, but like many values they exist on a spectrum and cultures embrace them to different degrees. For example, the countries from the continental European model are inclined toward conservatism and secrecy, whereas the Anglo-Saxon ones are inclined toward optimism and transparency.

TABLE 10.1 Gray's theoretical framework of cultural aspects of accounting

Accounting Values	Referring To	Characteristics
Conservatism vs. optimism	Measurement of assets, liabilities, and the financial result	Cautious approach to measurement in the face of uncertainty vs. more risk-taking approach
Secrecy vs. transparency	Information disclosures in a financial statement	Preference for disclosure of financial information about the business only to those closely involved in its management and financing vs. a more transparent, open, and publicly accountable approach

TABLE 10.2 Relationships between Gray's accounting values and Hofstede's cultural dimensions

Gray's Accounting Values	Hofstede's Cultural Dimensions					
	Power Distance	Individualism	Masculinity	Uncertainty Avoidance	Long-Term Orientation	Indulgence
Conservatism	Not identified	Lower	Lower	Higher	Higher	Lower
Secrecy	Higher	Lower	Lower	Higher	Higher	Lower

The relationships between Hofstede's cultural dimensions and Gray's (1988) conservatism and secrecy accounting values are shown in Table 10.2.

According to Gray (1988) and Radebaugh and Gray (2002), the more a culture wants to avoid uncertainty, looks at decisions and interactions as long term, and is more group-oriented and less competitive, the more likely they are to be conservative in their reporting, but also high in secrecy. For example, countries with high uncertainty avoidance and low individualism will be cautious in measurement of financial result and secretive in disclosures data in financial statements.

Cultural Contexts

The UK represents the Anglo-Saxon culture. In contrast to the UK, Poland is considered as an example of the continental European model of accounting. The main differences between the British and Polish accountants result from their mental preparation for adopting the IFRS spirit. The mentality of Poles—as in other nations—is historically rooted.

After the fall of communism in 1989, Poland began its transition from socialism to a market economy. Before 1989, the Polish accounting tradition was shaped by the needs of the centrally planned economy. The primary consumer of accounting information was the government which used this data as a mere tool of control and a source of statistical data for planning purposes. "In those years accounting constituted a very detailed set of rules" (Kosmala-MacLullich, 2003, p. 469) with no place for the concept of fair presentation in the financial statement. The preference for detailed and rigorous regulations as a consequence of strict adherence to the letter of the law that is rooted in this Polish mentality is not without influence on Polish accountants' decisions regarding IFRS application.

Second, the centrally planned economy is also characterized by the dominance of tax rules in accounting regulations. The fiscal system has been separated from financial accounting since 1994, when the first Accounting Act was introduced. However, entities are given a choice and still may apply accounting practices that reflect tax policy. The focus on tax issues frequently overshadows any other economic considerations and prevents the adoption of the IFRS perspective.

Third, the communist era has been a source of anti-market mentality and led to the formation of the "Homo Sovieticus" personality in Poland. The term "Homo Sovieticus" was introduced at the end of the 1980s by the Russian logician, philosopher, and writer Alexander Zinoviev and refers to a particular kind of mentality resulting from the influence of communist ideology (Tischner, 2018). Homo Sovieticus is deprived of initiative and critical-thinking spirit. Decisions depend on indications and orders from other people or institutions. What's more, the Homo Sovieticus personality is characterized by an inability to take individual action to solve problems and a fear of risk, which is characteristic of a conservative attitude. When Poland regained freedom in 1989, the changes in the economic system also required changes in human behavior, but the Homo Sovieticus did not automatically transform into a citizen of a democratic state (Wnuk-Lipinski, 2008).

In contrast, the UK took a different development path, which had a significant impact on the formation of separate social attitudes and its accounting ideology. The eighteenth century witnessed the beginning of the industrial revolution initiated in Great Britain. In the nineteenth century, the era of factory production and increasingly efficient and productive industrial civilization began, and economic activity was an individual matter. The formation of a capitalist mentality was observed and associated with a risk-taking attitude in the thinking of English businessmen (Motekat, 1965).

Hofstede-Gray Model for Poland and UK

This description of the Polish and UK cultural characteristics finds confirmation in the Hofstede-Gray theory of national culture (Table 10.3).

Except for the differences in the long-term orientation (LTO) dimension, differences in the other five cultural dimensions suggest that Polish accountants will be more conservative and secretive in their judgments than their British counterparts (Table 10.3). Poland, with an IND score of 60, is a less individualistic society than the UK (89 IND). These differences may be a result of the communist system where there was less preference for loosely knit social relations. Individuals tended to take care of only themselves and their immediate families.

Unlike the UK (35 UA), Poland is distinguished by a high preference for uncertainty avoidance (93 UA) and exhibits an emotional need for rules (even if the rules never seem to work). Security and risk aversion constitute important elements in individual motivation, which is characteristic of the Homo Sovieticus attitude (Gierusz et al., 2022).

Poland (64 MAS) ranks slightly lower than the UK (66 MAS) on masculinity. Societies with high masculinity score value attributes such as income, while the feminine ones tend to put relationships with people before money.

Poland's low score of 38 in the LTO dimension suggests that it should be more normative than pragmatic. Normative societies focus on a short-term perspective, consistent with a less conservative and secretive approach, where quick results and more disclosures in financial reports for investor decision-making are expected.

TABLE 10.3 Conversion of Hofstede data to Gray's conservatism and secrecy accounting values for Poland and the UK

Countries	Hofstede's Cultural Dimensions						Gray's Accounting Values	
	Power Distance (PDI)	Individualism (IND)	Uncertainty Avoidance (UA)	Masculinity (MAS)	Long-Term Orientation (LTO)	Indulgence (IVR)		
Poland	Higher	Lower	Higher	Lower	Lower	Lower	Conservatism	Secrecy
The UK	Lower	Higher	Lower	Higher	Higher	Higher	Optimism	Transparency

Polish culture with a score of 42 IVR can be characterized as restrained (opposite to indulgent). As such, contrary to the indulgent British culture (64 IVR), people tend to be cynical and pessimistic.

Regarding Gray's theory and the above characteristics of two cultures, we may presume that, contrary to their British counterparts, Polish accountants would be less likely to disclose information in financial reports "to preserve power inequalities" (due to higher PDI than for the UK) and to be more conservative in measurement and more secretive in disclosure. This would occur because Polish accountants are closely involved with the firm they work for and put emphasis on individual achievements (lower IND than for the UK). Polish accountants also have a high desire to preserve security (higher UA than for the UK). Polish accountants perceive earnings and achievements as less important and see themselves as constrained by social norms. For Polish accountants, indulgence, which would be reflected by making a decision that doesn't fully protect the potential future of the group, is wrong.

Polish Culture and the Interpretation of IFRS

Like the majority of EU countries, Poland started applying IFRS on a large scale on January 1, 2005. IFRS adoption meant that Polish accountants had to begin implementing the Anglo-Saxon model of accounting, and its embedded cultural values, thereby replacing the continental model of accounting and its inherent priorities.

IFRS create possibilities of choice for accountants. They are obliged to apply an approach which would be suitable for the circumstances—this is done on the basis of their own judgment. The vast majority of countries that have adopted IFRS have diverse national cultures, and IFRS adoption will not automatically change how people in a nation think. In view of the fact that judgments "are not made by automatons" (Salter et al., 2013, p. 608) but by accountants, cultural differences may cause accountants from various countries to interpret the same accounting standards differently. This, in turn, may result in an adverse impact on the intercultural comparability of financial statements.

National culture provides context for the many differences in accounting norms that persisted after IFRS adoption. One key area of difference can be found in the way national culture influences IFRS interpretation and disclosures in financial statements made by Polish and British accountants and how conservative and secretive the accounts were in their decision-making. Financial statement disclosures provide additional information about a company's financial operations. Disclosures are important because they provide stakeholders a better view into how financial decisions are made.

Two important areas in which culture could emerge in accounting decisions include the recognition of profit and loss as well as how disclosures are addressed within two different cultures.

IFRS Interpretation of Profit and Loss Recognition

One area where an accountant's culture may create a difference in interpretation is with the IFRS use of the term "probable", which happens frequently. This term is used consistently when talking about judgment to recognize profit or loss. For example, the IFRS states that the recognition of provision in a financial statement occurs when "the necessity of expenditure containing economic benefits for the purpose of settling obligations is probable" (IAS 37, Provisions, Contingent Liabilities and Contingent Assets, ¶14).

Accountants need to interpret the meaning of "is probable" and decide what that means. One accountant might decide that probability means over 50% likelihood, while another might consider over 60% to be probable. Different interpretations of this same expression by accountants—even in identical circumstances—might lead to different decisions. In turn, these decisions have an impact on the financial statements in terms of what information is provided. An accountant who opts for a lower probability threshold, for example, might choose to show the transactions resulting in recognition of profit/loss, whereas an accountant for whom that probability threshold is higher might not. Thus, the financial result of entities might be higher or lower even with identical initial data.

Taking the example of provisions treatment, let us assume that company X Ltd. is embroiled in a compensation lawsuit brought by company Y Ltd. X Ltd. may win or lose the lawsuit. If the X Ltd. loses the lawsuit, it will be obliged to pay compensation to Y Ltd. The accounting question is when is the right time to recognize the loss? A conservative accountant will need to be sure only for, let's say 50% to lose a lawsuit to recognize loss. An optimistic accountant, in a similar situation, will need to be sure for, let's say 80% to lose a lawsuit to record the loss. The financial results will vary depending on the approach applied. The conservative accountant will show the financial consequence sooner than will the optimistic accountant.

In light of Gray's theory, accountants who are conservative report the lowest value among possible alternative values for profits but the highest alternative values for losses. As mentioned in the previous section, the cultural characteristics of Poland and the UK suggest that Polish accountants will be more conservative than their British counterparts when interpreting accounting standards. Thus, Polish accountants, contrary to British accountants, will need greater certainty to recognize profit. Analogically,

Cultural Interpretation of IFRS in Accounting 139

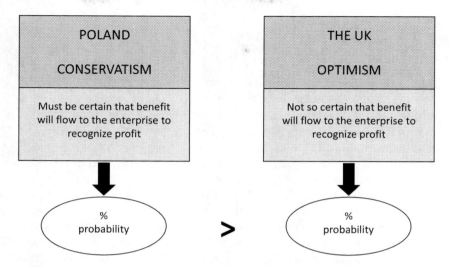

FIGURE 10.1 Conservatism vs. optimism and probability threshold for items increasing financial results (Gierusz et al., 2022)

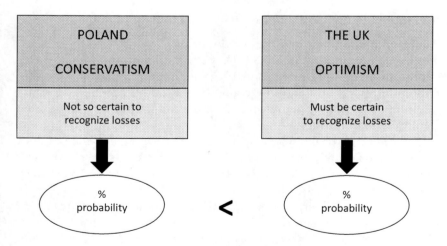

FIGURE 10.2 Conservatism vs. optimism and probability threshold for items decreasing financial results (Gierusz et al., 2022)

Polish accountants need lower certainty to recognize loss, contrary to British accountants. As such, Polish accountants will be more likely to delay net income increases, while accelerating net income decreases, compared to British accountants (Figures 10.1 and 10.2).

Following our example of provisions treatment, let's assume that the accountant from Poland works for Y Ltd., the company that has sued X Ltd. to pay compensation. The Polish accountant (represented as conservative) will need, let's say the certainty of 80% to recognize gain resulting from possible lawsuit win. If we assume the accountant is British (represented as optimistic), they will need, let's say the certainty of 50% to recognize gain resulting from possible lawsuit win. As a consequence, a Polish accountant will recognize the compensation gain *later* than their British counterpart.

Following the same example, now let's assume that the accountant from Poland works for X Ltd. that has been sued by company Y Ltd. The Polish accountant will need, let's say the certainty of 50% to recognize the financial loss resulting from possible loss of the lawsuit. If we assume that the accountant is British, they will need, let's say the certainty of 80% to recognize the financial loss resulting from the possible outcome of lawsuit. As a consequence, the Polish accountant would recognize the loss *sooner* than their British counterpart.

In sum, the Polish accountant would recognize and report financial losses sooner and financial gains later than would their British counterpart, thereby making the financial outlooks look very different, depending on the cultural interpretation.

IFRS Interpretation and Disclosures

The Anglo-Saxon culture should prioritize firm disclosures in financial statements prepared under IFRS if Gray's theory holds true. Anglo-Saxon cultural members value more transparency so they will be more likely to disclose information. Consequently, countries originating from the continental tradition of accounting are regarded as secretive, so they will be less likely to disclose information.

Referring to probability terms, an accountant who is regarded as more secretive should opt for a higher probability threshold, so they will need greater certainty to make disclosures than an accountant who is regarded as more transparent (Figure 10.3).

A contingent liability is a liability that may occur depending on the outcome of an uncertain future event (e.g., pending lawsuits or honoring product warranties). If you run a business, you need to be aware of the contingent liabilities that you have taken on. If the firm determines that the

MAKING OF DISCLOSURES IN THE FINANCIAL STATEMENT

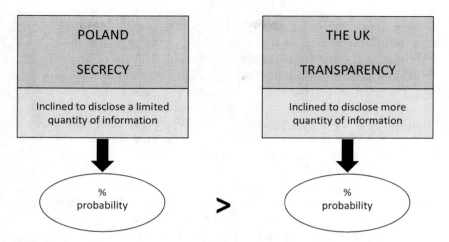

FIGURE 10.3 Secrecy vs. transparency and probability threshold for making disclosures in the financial statement (Gierusz et al., 2022)

likelihood of the liability occurring is remote, then the liability is only disclosed in a footnote of the financial statements. A Polish accountant would need, let's say the certainty of 30% to disclose such liability in a financial statement, whereas his British counterpart will need, let's say 10% to make this disclosure. As a consequence, the British accountant would disclose a higher quantity of such information in a financial statement.

So far, we have explored speculatively whether national culture may influence judgments made by Polish and British accountants when interpreting selected IFRS. However, we find little empirical support that Gray's accounting values of conservatism and secrecy affect this interpretation. With respect to the conservatism, the results in previous studies are mixed. For example, Hu, Chand, and Evans (2013) have found evidence that national culture may have an impact on accounting judgments. However, these studies addressed non-European countries. Other researchers including Wehrfritz and Haller (2014) and Chand, Cummings, and Patel (2012) find only some support for this notion.

In light of these cross-cultural studies, most of the available evidence is inconclusive, indicating the issue requires further investigation. As we have mentioned above, the Hofstede-Gray framework may have lost its explanatory power in cross-cultural research. Thus, perhaps researchers should explore other potentially powerful means of exploring culture, such as beliefs and norms (Kirkman, Lowe, & Gibson, 2017).

Conclusion

Nevertheless, we cannot eliminate cultural factors when examining accounting judgments in studies that include information related to firms from different countries. As researchers show, discernable national patterns in the use of IFRS continued after the 2005 adoption of IFRS in the EU (Guermazi & Halioui, 2020). Furthermore, the benefits of IFRS adoption were unevenly distributed among countries due to differences in institutions that operate in different cultures (Andre, 2017). Researchers have suggested applying alternative approaches for cross-cultural studies based on non-value aspects of culture, which could potentially explain the differences in accounting judgments better (Kirkman, Lowe, & Gibson, 2017; McSweeney, 2016).

National culture must be considered when examining the judgments made by accountants while making decisions. Despite the assumption that accounting is objective, there are a number of decisions that need to be made when reporting profit and loss and disclosing transactions. Polish and British cultures have historically different ideological perspectives, and those must be considered when interpreting selected IFRS.

Gray's (1988) model makes a stronger case for the difference between Polish and UK accounting differences, but scholars have since debated the extent to which cultural differences may influence accounting decisions (Chand, Cummings & Patel; 2012; Hu, Chand & Evans; 2013; Wehrfritz & Haller; 2014). As researchers have continued to study the question of conservatism and secrecy, they have found—perhaps because of global interaction and the creation of IFRS—some evidence of increasing similarity in accounting judgments. Studies addressing non-European countries persist in showing greater differences, but the continued interdependency of EU member countries, including citizen mobility, shared political discussions, and the ease of developing transnational corporations in the EU, has demonstrated the concept of culture as more fluid and diverse than national borders might imply. EU members may be less conservative after IFRS adoption than in the era of Gray's (1988) model (Salter & Lewis, 2011).

As national borders become less rigid and the world continues to develop multinational organizations, policies, and political agreements, cultural similarity may increase and the Hofstede-Gray framework may lose its explanatory power in cross-cultural research. However, international professionals should continue to expect worldview differences as well as other potentially powerful cultural differences such as beliefs and norms (Kirkman, Lowe, & Gibson, 2017). Cultures change slowly and anticipating difference means being aware of the multiple ways of thinking, even in a quantitative discipline like accounting.

Discussion Questions

- Why is culture important in explaining international differences in accounting?
- What is the relationship between Gray's accounting values and Hofstede's cultural dimensions?
- Why should the differences in IFRS interpretation be observed between Polish and British accountants?
- How would Polish accountants' need for higher certainty than their British counterparts influence the examples provided in terms of recognizing income?
- How would Polish accountants' need for lower certainty than their British counterparts influence the examples provided when recognizing loss?

Suggestions for Further Reading

Doupnik, T., & Richter, M. (2004). The impact of culture on the interpretation of in context verbal probability expressions. *Journal of International Accounting Research, 3*, 1–20.

Eljammi Ayadi, J., Damak, S., & Hussainey, K. (2020). The impact of conservatism and secrecy on the IFRS interpretation: The case of Tunisia and Egypt. *Journal of Financial Reporting and Accounting, 19*, 234–271.

Gierusz, J., Koleśnik, K., Silska-Gembka, S., & Zamojska, A. (2022). The influence of culture on accounting judgment – Evidence from Poland and the United Kingdom. *Cogent Business & Management, 9*(1). https://doi.org/10.1080/23311975.2021.1993556

Gray, S. J. (1988). Towards a theory of cultural influence on the development of accounting systems internationally. *Abacus, 24*, 1–15.

Hofstede, G., Hofstede, G. J., & Minkov, M. (2010). *Cultures and organizations: Software of the mind* (3rd ed.). New York: McGraw-Hill.

References

Andre, P. (2017). The role and current status of IFRS in the completion of European national accounting rules. *Accounting in Europe, 14*, 1–12.

Chand, P., Cummings, L., & Patel, C. H. (2012). The effect of accounting education of national culture on accounting judgments: A comparative study of Anglo-Celtic and Chinese culture. *European Accounting Review, 21*, 153–182.

Gierusz, J., Koleśnik, K., Silska-Gembka, S., & Zamojska, A. (2022). The influence of culture on accounting judgment – Evidence from Poland and the United Kingdom. *Cogent Business & Management, 9*(1). https://doi.org/10.1080/23311975.2021.1993556

Gray, S. J. (1988). Towards a theory of cultural influence on the development of accounting systems internationally. *Abacus, 24*, 1–15.

Guermazi, W., & Halioui, K. (2020). Do differences in national cultures affect cross-country conditional conservatism behavior under IFRS? *Research in International Business and Finance, 52*, 1–13.

Hartmann, B., Marton, J., & Andersson Sols, J. (2020). IFRS in national regulatory space: Insights from Sweden. *Accounting in Europe, 17,* 367–387.
Heidhues, E., & Patel, C. H. (2011). A critique of Gray's framework on accounting values using Germany as a case study. *Critical Perspectives on Accounting, 22,* 273–287.
Hofstede, G., Hofstede, G. J., & Minkov, M. (2010). *Cultures and organizations: Software of the mind* (3rd ed.). New York: McGraw-Hill.
Hu, C., Chand, P., & Evans, E. (2013). The effect of national culture, acculturation, and education on accounting judgments: A comparative study of Australian and Chinese Culture. *Journal of International Accounting Research, 12,* 51–77.
Kirkman, B. L., Lowe, K. B., & Gibson, C. B. (2017). A retrospective on culture's consequences: The 35-year journey. *Journal of International Business Studies, 48,* 12–29.
Kosmala-Maclullich, K. (2003), The true and fair view construct in the context of the Polish transition economy: Some local insights, *European Accounting Review, 12,* 465–487.
McSweeney, B. (2016). Collective cultural mind programming: Escaping from the cage, *Journal of Organizational Change Management, 29,* 68–80.
Motekat, U. K. (1965). Fundamental differences between Anglo-American and European accounting practices, *Woman C.P.A., 28*(1), 1.
Mueller, G., Gernon, H., & Meek, G. K. (1994). *Accounting: An international perspective, a supplement to introductory accounting textbooks.* IRWIN, Burr Ridge, IL, Boston, MA, Sydney, Australia.
Nobes, C. (2006). The survival of international differences under IFRS: Towards a research agenda. *Accounting and Business Research, 36,* 233–245.
Radebaugh, L. H., & Gray, S. J. (2002). *International accounting and multinational enterprises* (5th ed.). New York: John Wiley.
Salter, S. B., Kang, T., Gotti, G., & Doupnik, T. S. (2013). The role of social values, accounting values and institutions in determining accounting conservatism. *Management International Review, 53,* 607–632. https://doi.org/10 1007/s11575-012-0152-1
Salter, S. B., & Lewis, P. A. (2011). Shades of Gray: An empirical examination of Gray's model of culture and income measurement practices using 20-F data. *Advances in Accounting, 27,* 132–142.
Tischner, J. (2018). *Etyka Solidarności oraz Homo sovieticus* [Ethics of Solidarity and Homo Sovieticus]. Krakow: Wydawnictwo Znak.
Wehrfritz, M., & Haller, A. (2014). National influence on the application of IFRS: Interpretations and accounting estimates by German and British Accountants. *Advances in International Accounting, 30,* 196–208.
Wnuk-Lipinski, E. (2008). Dlugie pozegnanie. Homo sovieticus dzisiaj [Long farewell. Homo sovieticus today]. *Tygodnik Powszechny, 2.*

Conclusion

11
CULTURAL INFLUENCE AND ETHICAL CONSIDERATIONS FOR THE GLOBAL BUSINESS PROFESSIONAL

Mara K. Berkland and Amy Grim Buxbaum

We hope that the cases in this collection will help current and future global professionals recognize how distinctive cultural commitments are embedded in an array of different kinds of business interactions. From nonverbal subtleties in the hiring process to differences in global currency evaluation, the cross-cultural analyses presented here represent microcosms of global business interaction. Comparing different norms and expectations across disparate contexts reveals the diversity of priorities and values that professionals bring to international business relations. Each chapter presents an opportunity to surface the undercurrents of communication that must be negotiated whenever we interact with multicultural partners in a global economic system. After summarizing these contributions, in this final chapter we wish to take a moment to consider larger processes of cultural change and influence so that we might better appreciate what is potentially at stake whenever we engage in intercultural business communication. When we understand those stakes and gain some perspective on our own cultural orientations, our hope is that we might all be better able to make communicative choices that reflect more nuanced cultural understandings.

Review and Implications

We organized this volume by scope from the micro level to the meso level to the macro level in order to show how culture permeates business interactions throughout, between, and beyond organizations. Here, we highlight what we learned from each contribution and consider their implications.

DOI: 10.4324/9781003298199-16

In Chapter 2, Lao and Bencharit demonstrate the ways that expected performance of emotions influences hiring managers' decisions regarding potential employees. Given that the displays of emotion, in this case, an expression of enthusiasm versus an expression of composure, are laudable traits for subordinates and colleagues alike, the decision to prioritize one or the other consistently is culturally bound. Enthusiasm as a trait speaks more of a competitive nature, as enthusiasm is an assertive, forceful emotion, whereas composure reflects a prioritization of calm and stability. Both characteristics, again, are positive, and the consistent prioritizing of one over the other in a hiring process could, first, limit the diversity of employees hired, as Lao and Bencharit so clearly note, because composed, calm candidates might be overlooked. On a larger scale, selecting enthusiastic candidates over ones that exhibit calm has the capacity to shape larger professional practices and global communication norms.

In Chapter 3, Zhu explains how interactions are informally and formally moderated conversations, and specifically and how communicators perceive stops, starts, overlaps, and transitions while speaking in pairs and groups. In this piece, it is possible to see the arbitrary nature of codes. From one perspective, an interruption can spell a disrespect or disregard for a speaker's ideas or personhood. From another perspective, an interruption, or overlap, can communicate solidarity or support. As professionals negotiate the global landscape, Zhu rightly emphasizes that even small differences like these, even when all communicators interact with goodwill, can enable large conflicts.

In Chapter 4, Moon demonstrates the way the dimension of hierarchy/egalitarianism is manifest in professional communication. Communicators making requests of supervisors are influenced by their values, and as such, some professionals communicate deference to that value by acknowledging the weighted importance of their supervisors' time. The performance of deference to a supervisor coming from an egalitarian leaning culture would most likely seem kind or, at worst, timid or eccentric. Contrarily, the absence of communicated deference to a supervisor in a hierarchically leaning culture might be interpreted as an attempt to place oneself above group-oriented interests, spawning conflict, mistrust, and disharmony (Zhai, 2017).

In Chapter 5, Nishishiba clarifies that trust is very similarly gained within members of Japanese organizations and U.S. organizations, with one key difference—the prioritization of personal integrity or organizational commitment. The similarities are important to note, and both cultural groups valued responsible behavior, professional competence, and relational quality, which shows that professional behavioral expectations are more alike than different. At the same time, as Nishishiba clarifies, the prioritization of personal integrity over organizational commitment compels differences in a variety of professional norms such as those tied to overwork, absenteeism, network development, whistleblowing, creativity, teamwork, or conflict (Arumi, Aldrin, & Murti, 2019; Fitrio et al., 2019). In the end, this minor difference, as it is negotiated, represents a larger, ideological negotiation of the prioritization of groups or individuals. How this negotiation is settled, consciously or not, sets up future global professionals for expectations that will ultimately socialize what they, in turn, prioritize.

Looking at employee loyalty in Chapter 6, Meschke and Du illustrate distinct cultural differences between national cultures in terms of how employees see their supervisors and how they perceive overwork as indicative of company or team loyalty. As companies around the globe who have chosen to prioritize employee well-being and encourage work–life balance engage business partners from cultural perspectives in which the commitment to overwork is a symbol of trustworthiness, the potential for conflict or interpersonal resentment is great. Similarly, the quantity of expected work hours signals expected values for family and community interaction and even family and social structure. For example, who caretakes children or elder family members if extensive work hours are expected? Does this fall to other family members (which frequently ties to gender norms), or is the society at large expected to offer the infrastructure to care for those who need it (Annink, 2017; Cha, 2010; Leinonen, Solantaus, & Punamäki, 2003; Leung, 2014)? As cross-cultural interactions increase, the difference in expectations for workload will undoubtedly be points of tension.

In Chapter 7, Buxbaum and Berkland show how members of a multinational team harnessed their knowledge of their organization's national host culture in order to create a message that is critical of management and simultaneously establishes its own legitimacy to speak on the complex and difficult issue of sexual harassment. The power of multinational teams and workplaces is that diverse perspectives may emerge. Of course, that is only possible if the organization allows it and is not threatened by the changes elicited from the conversation. Unlike political democracies, economic organizations control "the type of information that is collected, how that information is arrayed and interpreted, and to whom it is disseminated" (Kerr, 2004, p. 85), limiting the true potential of multinational teams with complex and diverse knowledge sets and social viewpoints. Management is more likely to embrace such exchanges when the result is improved performance, but less likely to do so when the discourse puts itself at odds with the organizational values or structure. Organizations that allow employee input at multiple levels of decision-making risk questioning organizational values and beliefs, but also increase the potential for enrichment and growth (Stohl & Cheney, 2001).

Global tourism is increasingly important, and in Chapter 8, Berkland examines the layout of brick-and-mortar retail stores in Morocco and Norway and contributes to our understanding of about aesthetics, layout, pricing, and customer interaction, a conversation that scholars studying online retail are also having (Cheng, Thongma, & Wu, 2023; Kim, Yang, & Yong Kim, 2013; Thomas & Carraher, 2014). In this circumstance, the retail consumers, unlike global professionals, will likely have had less interaction with constituencies from different cultures since they are shopping from the comfort of their homes, and as such will be less likely to embrace different codes and norms in their shopping experiences. What this means is that adaptation will consistently be made to consumers with the most capital, as the purpose of retail is to sell.

In Chapter 9, Mason and Dasgupta provide a cultural perspective on economic activity. Cash is a tool used within culture to mitigate uncertainty and risk, in that it is anonymous and within the holder's immediate control. For countries with large shadow economies, cash is highly valued and widely used. As banking, credit, and cryptocurrencies are competing within the global market, cash presents a potential obstacle for those financial platforms as, ultimately, the question for currency users is the level of control they are allowed (Busse et al., 2020; Cristofaro et al., 2023). It is worth stating that the political and organizational trust that would be required to create a global currency system is immense, and local currency users would need significant incentive to embrace it.

In Chapter 10, Koleśnik and Silska-Gembka examine the norms and values that emerge after global professional standards are set. Specifically, they examine the differences between reporting standards by accountants in different countries. In contrast to most of the chapters in this text, Koleśnik and Silska-Gembka find that cultural differences predicted by Gray (1988) did not, or perhaps, no longer, hold. Gray's research emerged in the late 1980s, before the adoption of a set of international reporting standards. The implementation of a global standard or system is meant to create uniformity, clarity, and consistency. Although scholars were not able to continually test Gray's (1988) accounting values across cultures before the International Financial Reporting Standards (IFRS) were applied broadly in 2005, it is likely that a set of globally embraced norms would bring adopting nations closer, rather than farther apart, in how they interpret reporting expectations.

Although each chapter focuses on a unique context and highlights different cultural orientations, together they demonstrate how cross-cultural dimensions cut across professional contexts. Despite good intentions to be open and aware, global business professionals always carry with them their national, organizational, and disciplinary socializations and bring those expectations to interactions. Becoming more aware of the nuanced layering of cultural orientations across organizational levels is critical to developing cultural competence in business settings large and small.

Moreover, in recent decades, technological innovation has catapulted global professional interactions from occasional, high-stress, resource-intense events to everyday phenomena. The benefits of such frequent engagements with professionals from outside of our cultures of origin is the chance to engage new ideas, languages, ways of interacting, products, processes, and materials. In the frenzy of commerce, the prioritization of efficiency and the power of need may prevent thoughtful negotiation of the ways business gets done and the priorities and values embedded in those decisions. Certainly, efficiency and clarity are key factors in decision-making. Resources are not infinite, regardless of the success of the organization, and that must be taken into account when making business decisions. At the same time, it is imperative for global professionals to weigh potential long-term consequences of immediate decisions to make sure that the values are in line with the system in which they would like to work, rather than the system that, at least in the moment, feels the most familiar or is easiest to execute.

Interpersonal, organizational, and institutional practices are also opportunities to form current and future priorities. As global professionals recognize the power of their choices, even in small interactions, they can understand how each instance of intercultural communication is a negotiation of cultural priorities and values. The processes, expectations, performances, and communication styles we negotiate have the potential to impact all decisions that come after, even if only in a small way. In this way, global professionals are not just charged with enacting commercial exchanges for the good of their company or their career but are participating in the co-creation of a global commerce system under which they and others will be expected work in the future. Understanding cultural influence and change, and our ethical obligations in a global business context, can help us to participate in a culturally mindful way.

Cultural Change and Influence

Complicating our understanding of culture is the fact that it is not static, but rather is constantly evolving. Because the cultural system relies on consistency and common understanding in order to function coherently, cultural changes do not take shape quickly. The introduction of even a small change takes time to catch and spread throughout a culture. Such shifts may seem monumental to those within a system, but, when compared with the array of cultural options that exist across the globe, change normally manifests in small increments. What may feel like a big difference between two people or groups, when put into context of the array of global options available for ideology, values, norms, and codes, they may actually be quite similar.

Three characteristics of culture make it vulnerable to change. First, culture allows people who share a place and time to efficiently function together. It is a system that allows people to coordinate their actions so that resources can be shared and the members of the group can persist. In order for its people to survive, then, culture necessarily must be responsive. When the systemic norms and codes no longer facilitate efficient or effective interaction, the system will adjust. As its environment changes, culture adapts to new needs, constraints, or influences.

Second, cultural borders are fluid and permeable, and overlap with other cultural systems. The edges of a culture are constantly exposed to the ideologies, values, norms, and codes of a different system, which means that interactions that take place on the borders must be comprehensible in both systems. As the cultural thresholds absorb or adapt to systemic components of the neighboring system, those exposures can trickle through to the dominant culture.

Third, humans have never been geographically bound. Historically, humans have entered new cultural systems for the purpose of resource control, trade, or tourism. As individuals or groups migrate or simply even visit another cultural system, they bring their ideologies, values, norms, and codes, which may be adopted and adapted by the people they encounter in the new culture. In the process, they too are exposed to new ideologies, values, norms, and codes, and may introduce some of them into their base system.

However, not all of these newly introduced cultural practices will take hold. When confronted with an unfamiliar or contested perspective, cultures can either accept it and make a small transformation or reject it in favor of the status quo. Often, a cultural system will only transform in small increments, because any abrupt changes in the system might impact the functioning of other components. At the same time, once an idea is introduced, the culture will now have the new concept or way of being in its consciousness, where it might not have been before, and so no return to normal is never quite complete.

Three key factors can influence cultural change: need, repetition, and trust. Need is the greatest factor predicting whether a cultural system will evolve and adopt a new cultural perspective or behavior. The purpose of any system is to achieve an outcome in a way that uses cultural or material resources efficiently and effectively. The greater need that a culture has, especially to meet basic survival needs, the more likely it is to take on new ways of thinking and interacting. A simple example would be collecting water. If a culture's traditional way of collecting water no longer yields water, or if there is a way to collect cleaner water, more water, or geographically closer water, it is highly likely the culture will embrace the new water collection method. The cultural system will respond and evolve to better meet the need.

In addition, the more repetitive exposure a group has to a new systemic component, the more likely the cultural system will absorb and integrate it. When group members repeatedly see a norm or symbol or are told that a value or perspective is important, the more familiar that concept or behavior will become. Desensitization to the concept over time fosters familiarity that may ultimately allow it to be integrated into the cultural system. Finally, how much cultural members trust or need the person/people performing the unfamiliar norm, using the new symbol, or reflecting a different value or worldview will influence whether and how that new element is accepted. Liking, trusting, or needing the source of the new cultural component will impact the degree to which a cultural system will integrate any new or different ways of being they introduce.

Understanding the dynamic and permeable nature of culture helps us to conceptualize business interactions and transactions in a wider ethical context. Ethically, there is much to consider when entering into an intercultural dialogue, especially when one considers the intervening and omnipresent factor of power in professional business interactions. When an organization is situated within the boundaries of a national culture that may not have the resources or infrastructure to fully support its people, cultural norms may be sacrificed in order to adapt to a business partner that presents them with needed resources. A consequence of such adaptation is the decrease in cultural diversity around the globe, not only in terms of languages but in terms of values and ideologies.

Globalization and Cultural Adaptation: Ethical Considerations

As products, services, people, and ideas move more freely across the globe, cultures change (Bird & Stevens, 2003). Globalization, at its core, is not just about "selling internationally, or having offices, production facilities and warehouses in numerous locations throughout the world" (McCann, 1998, p. 2), but it requires the creation and acceptance of a cohesive economic and commerce system. A global commerce system needs to effectively allow for the exchange of goods and services: "it is an economy with the capacity to work as a unit in real time on a planetary scale" (Marković, 2008, p. 4).

Likewise, global professionals require a shared symbol or code system in order to effectively execute their business transactions. *Lingua franca* is the term used to refer to a common bridge or trade language that serves to facilitate communication between people who speak different languages. Fluency in the *lingua franca* is thus an imperative for participants in global commerce. In addition to providing a common language, *lingua franca* "has served as media for the transmission of cultural, social, and professional knowledge, assisted in the formation of global-local power structures, and functioned as shibboleths for determining friend from foe" (Ding & Saunders, 2006, p. 3). Because language is inextricably linked to culture as it reflects and reaffirms the affiliated ideological system, *lingua franca* enables and constrains what can be said, what ways of being and interacting are prioritized, and the way relationships form.

The current *lingua franca* for global business interactions is English, meaning that even in interactions between professionals with no native speakers of English, the language used is frequently English. As sets of symbols, English languages reflect the values and ideologies of the cultures in which they are spoken natively. Those who learn the *lingua franca* of English thus learn its embedded values and ideals as the language binds the speaker to the limits of the ideas within the language and also introduces ideas and concepts never experienced in their native tongue (Kramsch, 1998).

Although a commerce system serves to facilitate economic exchange, culturally it is not value-free. As more newcomers are invited to participate and are socialized into the global economic arena by learning its norms and codes, they will be exposed and implicitly encouraged to embrace new values and ideologies. On its surface, this may not seem problematic, but in some cases, those ideological frames will sit in opposition to the priorities and values from one's own culture. A global business professional will be expected to negotiate that conflict; understanding what cultural factors are in play may help them to better navigate the tension. Moreover, such socialization is not without impact. When a person learns a new norm or is urged to embrace a new system of codes, they will be changed intellectually, if nothing else. When the global professional returns to the organization or national culture of origin, the values and ideologies are likely to trickle in, creating change and influence that might be unanticipated or even unwelcome.

The mere existence of a shared system should prompt global professionals to consider which norms and codes are in use, how they are chosen, and what are the implications for individuals and cultures alike. These questions are important to unpack because "power is an omnipresent but often hidden part of all intercultural interactions" (Martin, Flores, & Nakayama, 2002, p. 366). Those with less power have more need for an interaction to be successful. Whether the need is economic, political, or social, the position of less power and greater dependence means cultural vulnerability, which increases the likelihood of adaptation. Because of this need to adapt, those with less power often understand the powerful better than the powerful understand them. This creates a circumstance where the people who are already culturally adapted consider their system as "correct" or "normal" and may struggle to see other ways of being as legitimate or lack the skills to think or act differently.

Who adapts to whom and the subsequent economic, political, or social systems that become normalized at a global level are not thoughtfully chosen based on merit. Rather, cultural systems become normalized out of need or adherence to precedent. If one group needs something urgently or considerably, it becomes incumbent upon it to adapt to the language and norms of the group who possesses the resource. The need in question can be physical, social, political, economic, or spiritual. For example, if one culture needs military support or access to an environmental resource, the group that will adapt is the one who most needs the interaction to be successful. Once a pattern and common understanding are established, and a number of members of a community have adapted to a specific language, economic, and social system, precedent becomes the predictor of which system will be employed in later interactions. As members of the global business community began to speak the language to adapt to U.S. professionals, politicians, and media, English became the *lingua franca*. Today, so many people speak English that it has become a global language. In fact, many scholars argue that English will be the globe's last *lingua franca*, and instead we will see the proliferation of Englishes: English, with its embedded norms and values, becomes intertwined with other languages at the local levels creating hybrid ways of interacting (Gao, 2021; Kankaanranta & Lu, 2013).

What is seldom asked in the negotiation of *lingua franca*, shared economic systems, or social norms is "What ideology is being prioritized?" or "What values are represented in the norms or symbols we are currently using?" or "How will the process we have chosen constrain what we can or cannot do?" Would global professionals want a system that prioritizes the health of many over competition? Is long-term thinking, rather than short-term goals, more important? Is efficiency more important than relationships? Is linguistic clarity more important than linguistic beauty? No one linguistic, economic, nor social system can provide every option, yet the repetition of norms for commerce have created a global system that has ideological imperatives that are very difficult to counter.

Each instance of intercultural communication is a micro-level negotiation of the priorities and values that will be normalized in global interactions. Which process, expectation, performance, or communication style is embraced has the capacity to become precedent and that impacts subsequent interactions. In this way, global professionals aren't merely "doing their jobs" as they work with people from different cultures. Each interaction presents an opportunity to negotiate cultural understandings. Clarifications of global standards aren't just about norms, but about values and ideologies. In addition to questions like "What is clear?" or "What is efficient?" even at the micro level, professionals have the responsibility to ask "What do we prioritize?" and "Who do we—the global business community—want to be?"

International business professionals may feel that their role is tiny, that they are merely small cogs in a giant global machine, but we believe that becoming more interculturally competent can provide hope rather than resignation. The key is to conceive of our global professional interactions as part of a larger cultural ecosystem that allows participants to see their potential influence. One exposure in an ecosystem, such as introducing a new component or modifying a traditional way of interacting, will change the elements around it. Even if the new exposure simply sets forth a new concept, that is a change in the options and perspectives the ecosystem now has available, which in turn creates the possibility of its implementation at a different point. For example, a global professional who asks in a meeting, "Why are we focusing so much on this employee candidate's enthusiasm? What is it that we are looking for or what might we be missing by prioritizing it?" draws attention to that decision, making it seem less natural or taken for granted. Similarly, supervisors who reward overwork are making decisions that impact the larger social system beyond the organization. As they encourage or discourage such behavior in their teams, they are sending messages to those employees and those who interact with the employees what a laudable value is.

In sum, global business professionals are explorers in the global ecosystem, and the decisions they make daily will have effects that last longer than the consequences of those immediate decisions. The policy drafted today might be embraced moving forward. The meeting norms modeled by a manager might be repeated or held as a standard for the employees in the future. Each decision is a socializing one, and as such, each global professional has the power to influence the larger global system under which we all might operate someday.

Discussion Questions

- The chapters in this volume present a variety of cultural interpretations of ideal professional interactions. Which perspectives are, from your perspective, worthy of integrating into global professional norms? Why?
- What are some examples of the ways global professionals have embraced dominant cultural norms that might not serve every interaction?

- What might you be able to do, as a future professional, to engage, and perhaps adapt to, perspectives from other cultures?
- What values do you believe should undergird global professional interactions? Why?

References

Annink, A. (2017). From social support to capabilities for the work–life balance of independent professionals. *Journal of Management & Organization, 23*(2), 258–276.

Arumi, M. S., Aldrin, N., & Murti, T. R. (2019). Effect of organizational culture on organizational citizenship behavior with organizational commitment as a mediator. *International Journal of Research in Business and Social Science (2147-4478), 8*(4), 124–132.

Bird, A., & Stevens, M. J. (2003). Toward an emergent global culture and the effects of globalization on obsolescing national cultures. *Journal of International Management, 9*(4), 395–407.

Busse, K., Tahaei, M., Krombholz, K., von Zezschwitz, E., Smith, M., Tian, J., & Xu, W. (2020, September). Cash, cards or cryptocurrencies? A study of payment culture in four countries. In *2020 IEEE European Symposium on Security and Privacy Workshops (EuroS&PW)* (pp. 200–209). Piscataway, NJ: IEEE.

Cha, Y. (2010). Reinforcing separate spheres: The effect of spousal overwork on men's and women's employment in dual-earner households. *American Sociological Review, 75*(2), 303–329.

Cheng, F. F., Thongma, W., & Wu, C. S. (2023). The influence of website social cues: A cross-culture comparison. *Journal of Computer Information Systems, 63*(2), 351–368.

Cristofaro, M., Giardino, P. L., Misra, S., Pham, Q. T., & Hiep Phan, H. (2023). Behavior or culture? Investigating the use of cryptocurrencies for electronic commerce across the USA and China. *Management Research Review, 46*(3), 340–368. https://doi.org/10.1108/MRR-06-2021-0493

Ding, S., & Saunders, R. A. (2006). Talking up China: An analysis of China's rising cultural power and global promotion of the Chinese language. *East Asia, 23*(2), 3–33.

Fitrio, T., Apriansyah, R., Utami, S., & Yaspita, H. (2019). The effect of job satisfaction to organizational citizenship behavior (OCB) mediated by organizational commitment. *International Journal of Scientific Research and Management, 7*(9), 1300–1310.

Gao, F. (2021). Negotiation of native linguistic ideology and cultural identities in English learning: A cultural schema perspective. *Journal of Multilingual and Multicultural Development, 42*(6), 551–564. https://doi.org/10.1080/01434632.2020.1857389

Gray, S. J. (1988). Towards a theory of cultural influence on the development of accounting systems internationally. *Abacus, 24,* 1–15.

Kankaanranta, A., & Lu, W. (2013). The evolution of English as the business lingua franca: Signs of convergence in Chinese and Finnish professional communication.

Journal of Business and Technical Communication, 27(3), 288–307. https://doi.org/10.1177/10506519134799

Kerr, J. L. (2004). The limits of organizational democracy. *Academy of Management Perspectives, 18*(3), 81–95.

Kim, J., Yang, K., & Yong Kim, B. (2013). Online retailer reputation and consumer response: Examining cross cultural differences. *International Journal of Retail & Distribution Management, 41*(9), 688–705.

Kramsch, C. (1998). *Language and culture*. Oxford: Oxford University Press.

Leinonen, J. A., Solantaus, T. S., & Punamäki, R. L. (2003). Social support and the quality of parenting under economic pressure and workload in Finland: The role of family structure and parental gender. *Journal of Family Psychology, 17*(3), 409.

Leung, L. C. (2014). Gender mainstreaming childcare policy: Barriers in a Confucian welfare society. *Journal of International and Comparative Social Policy, 30*(1), 41–52.

Marković, M. R. (2008). Managing the organizational change and culture in the age of globalization. *Journal of Business Economics and Management, 9*(1), 3–11.

Martin, J., Flores, L., & Nakayama, T. (2002). Ethical issues in intercultural communication. In J. Martin, T. Nakayama, & L. Flores (Eds.), *Readings in intercultural communication: Experiences and contexts* (2nd ed., pp. 363–371). New York: McGraw-Hill.

McCann, J. M. (1998). *Globalization: Real time relationships among dispersed individuals and organizations.* http://participationage.wordpress.com/what-is-globalization

Stohl, C., & Cheney, G. (2001). Participatory processes/paradoxical practices: Communication and the dilemmas of organizational democracy. *Management Communication Quarterly, 14*(3), 349–407.

Thomas, T., & Carraher, C. E. (2014). A retail perspective on the shopping behavior, cultures and personalities for China, United Arab Emirates, Belgium, India, Germany and America. *Journal of Technology Management in China, 9*(3), 289–296.

Zhai, Y. (2017). Values of deference to authority in Japan and China. *International Journal of Comparative Sociology, 58*(2), 120–139.

INDEX

Note: **Bold** page numbers refer to tables; *Italic* page numbers refer to figures and page numbers followed by "n" denote endnotes.

accessibility/receptivity 62, 113
accounting 130; Anglo-Saxon model of 130, 137; conservatism *vs.* optimism *139*; continental model of 130; cultural influence and 131–134; financial accounting 134; Gray's theoretical framework **132**; Hofstede—Gray model 135–137; planned economy 134; principles-based approach 130; secrecy *vs.* transparency *141*
Accounting Act 134
accounting values 132, **133**, **136**, 141, 150
adjacency pair 35, 40, 43
adjusting concept 120
affect valuation theory (AVT) 23–24
age 54–55
American English: cultural contexts 36–37; turn-taking behavior 41; turn-taking protocol 37–40
anti-market mentality 134
apology: concept of 51–52; expression of 53; function of 51
Argentina: cash demand 118; CIC/GDP ratio 125; denomination 125; economies balance 120; financial emergency 126; inflation 124–125; new currency notes 124–125; uncertainty dimension 120
ascription/achievement dimension 10
Asian Americans 21, 25, 27–28
automated teller machines (ATMs) 118

banks 118–119
Barber, Bernard 61
behavioral pattern 53, 76
Bencharit, Lucy Zhang 15, 148
Berkland, Mara K. 15, 16, 149, 150
"Bipartite Employee Loyalty" (BEL) approach 75
Brown, P. 51, 55
business communication 61
business professionals 14; cross-cultural interactions 3, 14; global ecosystem 156
Buxbaum, Amy Grim 15, 149

capital markets 131
cash demand: banks 118–119; comparison 120–123; credit and banks 125–127; cultural

160 Index

considerations 127–128; inflation 118
cash holdings 120
Chand, P. 141
Chinese working adults 29
Chinese workplace culture 80
closed-mouth smiles 23
code, cultural systems 5–6
code of ethics 68
collectivism 63, 75; *vs.* individualism 47
collectivist orientation 9, 63, 69
communication styles 8, 11, 46–47, 50, 54, 65, 76; behaviors 62; breakdown 36; cultural differences 47, 55; definition of 46
communism 134
Confucianism 46, 82; cultural ethos 47; work ethics 80
Conservatism 131, 132; *vs.* optimism *139*
contextual factors 41–43
contingent liability 140
corralito 126
Covarrubias, P. O. 8
credit and banks 125–127
credit cards 119
cross-cultural communication 4
cross-cultural differences 83; emotions in work settings 22
cross-cultural interactions 3, 8, 16
cross-cultural professional interactions 13–14
cross-cultural practice 40–41
cross-language practice 40–41
cultural contexts 24–25; American english 36–37; Germany and China 76; Mandarin Chinese 36–37; South Korea 48; United Kingdom 48; United States 48
cultural differences in politeness 4, 55, 64–65; in email communication 48–49; in emotions 25; as function of status relations 49–51; gratitude expression use 52–54; trustworthiness 70; use of apology and culture 51–52
cultural dimensions 107, 132; employee loyalty effects 75–76; uncertainty avoidance 119
cultural fit 21

cultural systems 4–5; code 5–6; cultural socialization 7; ideology 6–7; norms 6; unique cultural systems 7; values 6
cultural tourism 105; authentic experience of 113; cultural dimensions 106–107; cultural goods 106
cultural value dimensions 8, 52, 106
culture/cultural: accommodation 42; adaptation 153–156; borders 152; change and influence 151–153, 152; characteristics of 152; communication styles 46–47, 49; competence 3; complex components of 4; considerations 127–128; elements of 5; ideological framework 4; individualism/collectivism 63; non-value aspects of 142; peculiarity 75; sensitivity 3; socialization 7; subsystems 7; uncertainty avoidance dimension 106–107
Cummings, L. 141
currency 117; exchange 15; factors affecting 120; GDP fraction *vs.* savings deposits *121*
currency in circulation (CIC) 122
customer interaction 114, 150

Dasgupta, Kabir 16, 150
debit cards 118, 119
decision-making 6, 137
defense, loyalty 80
demographic diversity 21
demonetization policy 123–124
deposits, protection of 118
digital payment technologies 119
dignity cultures 47
direct communication styles 46–47, 49
dominant cultural group 7
Du, Juana 15, 149

East Asian cultures 24, 52, 55
Eastern cultures: employee loyalty 75; face approach 80; social harmony 80
economic exchange 117
economic system 135
economic transaction 68

Index **161**

egalitarianism 10
egalitarian-leaning cultures 90
email advertisements 52
email communication style 45, 48, 50
emotional labor 22
emotions: cultural differences 25; hiring managers' decisions 148; independence 63; information 110; physical expression of 27–28; signaling emotions in interviews 29–30; in work settings 22; writing emotions in résumés 28–29
employee loyalty 74, 148; concept of 75; cross-cultural differences 83; for East Asian cultures **79**; Eastern cultures 75; effects of 75–76; employee behavior 75; exploratory factor analysis 77; negative behaviors 76; with negative outcomes (Chinese) 79; with negative outcomes (German) **78**; Western cultures 75
employees: behavior 75; emotions in work settings 22; health 76; unsafe environment for 96
employers: and culture value 24; ideal emotion 29; job applicants selection 21; unconscious bias 21
enthusiasm expression 148
equality 97–99
ethnicity 21
European Americans 27; calm applicant 29; smile intensity *27*; value excitement states 31
European Union (EU) 131
Evans, E. 141
extended concurrent speech 37

face: approach 75, 80; culture 47; *vs.* dignity 47; face-saving strategy 45–46; face-threatening acts 51
facework strategies 52
facial expressions *30*
fairness and dignity 62, 96–97
fair presentation concept 134
familiarity 106
financial accounting development 132
financial security 63

formal communication styles 49
formal employment contract 74
French-German model of accounting 130

Gallup survey 89–90
gender 21; equality 90; identification 21
geographic boundaries 8
Germany: conversation culture 80; employee loyalty 75, 78; fact- and rule-oriented 76; health-care organizations 76
global accounting system 131
global commerce system 153
global economic system 147
globalization 10, 131, 153–156
Global Leadership and Organizational Behavior Effectiveness (GLOBE) dimensions 8
global tourism 16
global virtual teams (GVTs) 11
Goffman, E. 45
goods and services: exchange of 153; inflation 118; market-based transactions of 127; presentation of 111–112
gratitude concept 52–53
Gray, S. J. 132–134, 142, 150
gross domestic product (GDP) 117, *121*
group identity 64
group orientation 75, 81
guanxi 82

Hall, B. J. 8
Hall, E. 11
Haller, A. 141
hard-work ethic 68
hierarchy/egalitarian dimension 9–10
high arousal positive (HAP) states 23
high-context/low-context dimension 11–12
high-intensity smile 28
hiring process: affect valuation theory 23–24, 31; cultural contexts 24–25; discrimination 21; emotional diversity in 24; hiring decision 30–31; job application process 25–30; racial and gender identification 21
Hofstede, G. 8, 107, 119

"Homo Sovieticus" personality 134–135
Hong Kong (HK) Chinese 27; facial expressions 30; smile intensity 27; written responses 26
Hu, C. 141

ideal emotions 24, 25, 27
ideology, cultural systems 6–7
income, definition of 122
income-generating economic exchanges 117
income payments 118
India: cash demand 118; CIC/GDP ratio 122; demonetization policy 123–124; economies balance 120; Indian monetary authority 124; labor market disruptions 124; *Pradhan Mantri Jan Dhan Yojana* 126; shadow economy 123–124; *Tirumala Tirupati Venkateswara* temple 129n1; uncertainty dimension 120
indirect communication styles 46, 49
individualism 47, 63; *vs.* collectivism 9, 62–64
Individualism Distance Index (IDV) 48
individualist culture 63
individualist orientation 69
"indulgence/restraint" dimension 80
industrial revolution 130, 135
inequality degree 90
inflation 118
informal sector 117
integrity 62, 68–69
intercultural business communication 9, 16, 37, 49, 147
interdependent view of trustworthiness 69
International Financial Reporting Standards (IFRS) 130–131, 150; interpretation and disclosures 140–141; profit and loss recognition 138–140
interpersonal communication 45, 52; face-saving strategy 45–46
interpersonal conflicts 55
interpersonal interaction 15
interpersonal relationships 76, 82
interruption 36
ittaikan (feeling oneness) 64

Jacobsen, H. 89
Japan: business contexts 64; collectivist orientation 64; trustworthiness concept 64
Japanese businesspeople 65; organizational commitment 65; trustworthiness concept 69; trustworthiness groupings 66
Japanese conceive integrity 69
Japanese corporation 65
Japanese society 63–64
Jefferson, G. 37, 41
job application process: emotions, physical expression of 27–28; signaling emotions in interviews 29–30; writing emotions in résumés 28–29; written responses 25–27

Kirschbaum, K. A. 8
Koleśnik, Katarzyna 16, 150
Korean language 54–55
Koreans' polite behavior 48

labor market disruptions 124
Lao, Chi Cheng 15, 148
legitimacy, sexual harassment: equality 97–99; fairness and dignity 96–97; safe working environment 95–96
Levinson, S. C. 51, 55
li ("propriety") 82
Lian, H. 10
Lingua franca 153–155
linguistic rules 37
long-term orientation (LTO) dimension 135
low arousal positive (LAP) states 23
low-context communication styles 11, 46, 91
loyalty 62; Chinese conceptualizations of 78–80; defense 80; employee conceptualizations of 76; expression 67; German conceptualizations of 76–78; healthy degree of 75; managerial strategies 82–84; overwork 80–81; supervisors perception 81–82

management styles 10
managerial strategies 82–84

Mandarin Chinese: cultural contexts 36–37; sociocultural context of 42; turn-taking protocol 36–37
Mason, Brenden J. 16, 150
mastery/adaptive dimension 12–13
mental health outcomes 22
Meschke, Stephan 15, 149
#MeToo movement 87, 90
Minkov, M. 119
miscommunication 15
monochronic/polychronic dimension 12
Moon, Chanki 15, 148
moral conduct 82
Morocco: brick-and-mortar retail stores 150; Moroccan-style leather products 109; retail aesthetics in 108–110; shopping experience 113
multicultural organization 90–91

national accounting systems 130
national cultures 7; definition of 8; ideological frameworks of 8; worldview orientations 13
national employee loyalty 76
negative emotions 22, 24, 25
negative face 45, 51
Netherlands 87, 90
new currency notes 124–125
Nishishiba, Masami 15, 148
nonverbal behaviors 10
nonverbal expressions 27
non-Western countries 22
norms, cultural systems 6
Norway: Finmark region of 110; indigenous culture 110; retail aesthetics in 110–111; Sami art and jewelry 110–111
novelty 106

openness 62
organizations: commitment 65–68; contexts 74, 83; cultures 7; loyalty 15, 77, 78; psychological safety within 90
Otterbach, S. 90
overlap concept 36
overwork, loyalty 80–81

paper checks 118
Patel, C. H. 141

people of color 21
performance indicators 61
personal initiative 63
personal integrity 64, 68–69, 148
person's self-image 63
pleasure seeking 63
Poland: Hofstede—Gray model 135–137; IFRS interpretation 137–140; secrecy accounting values **136**
politeness strategy: cultural differences in 48–49; as face-saving strategy 45–46; factors 54–55; individual's communication styles 48; interpersonal relationships 47; politeness behavior 45
politeness theory 55
political structures 8
positive emotions 24, 29
positive face 45, 51
positive social value 45
power distance dimension 47, 54, 90
Power Distance Index (PDI) 48
practitioners, implications for 70
pragmatic strategy 41
predictability/consistency 62
pricing 112–113
product education 113–114
professional communication 148
professional competence 65
professional contexts 10
professional culture 7
profit and loss recognition 138–140
promise fulfillment 62
Protestant work ethic 68
psychological contract theory 74, 83
psychological risk 113

race 21
Radebaugh, L. H. 134
receptivity **64**
relational distance 54
relational quality 65
reliability/dependability 62
ren ("benevolence") 82
responsibility 64
responsible behavior 65
retail aesthetics: goods, presentation of 111–112; in Morocco 108–110; in Norway 110–111; pricing 112–113; product

education 113–114; shopping concerns 114–115; uncertainty avoidance 111
right to privacy 63
risk-avoidant shoppers 112

Sacks, H. 37, 41
safe working environment 95–96
Sami art and jewelry 110–111
savings deposits, interest rate *121*
savings in bank account 123
Schegloff, E. A. 36, 37, 41
secrecy accounting values 134
secrecy *vs.* transparency *141*
self-assessment/presentation 48
self-criticism 48
self-selection technique 34
sexual harassment 15, 87, 88–89, 149; allegations, email exchange 91–94; cultural context 90–91; definition of 88; Gallup survey 89–90; multicultural organization 90–91; unwelcome sexual behaviors 88–89
shadow economy 117, 123–124
shadow market 118
shagun, cash gifts 127
Shaw, R. B. 68
shopping concerns 114–115
shopping tourism 105
Shozan Suzuki 65
Sigal, J. 89
sign systems *see* code, cultural systems
Silska-Gembka, Sylwia 16, 150
Singaporean students 22
Singelis, T. M. 63
smile intensity: European American *vs.* HK Chinese *27*
social harmony 75, 80
socialism 134
social mobility 10
social structures 8
sociocultural context 41
socio-emotional cues 5
socio-hierarchical contexts 51
sole cultural dimension 47
Sousa-Poza, A. 90
souvenirs 106
subjective decision-making 114
substantial monetary support 105
Sullivan, J. J. 68
supervisor loyalty 78
supervisors perception 81–82

tax assessment 131
time management and punctuality 76
tourism 105, 150; cultural values 106; international retail interactions 106–107; risk, types of 107; shopping tourism 105; substantial monetary support 105; tourist behaviors 106; worldview dimension 107
tourist: behaviors 106; consumption characteristics 107–108; negotiation processes 108; purchases and uncertainty 107–108
traditional Zen Buddhism 67
transition relevance place (TRP) 34
travel shopping 107
"Tripartite Employee Loyalty" (TEL) 75, 80
trust 61; conceptualization of 61–62; cultural differences 64–65; dimensions of 68; Japan and United States 64; organizational contexts 61
trustworthiness: concept of 69; conceptualization of 61–62; cultural dimensions 62–64; independent views 69; individualism *vs.* collectivism 62–64; interdependent 69; Japanese concept of 69; organizational commitment 65–68; personal integrity 65, 68–69; practitioners, implications for 70; professional competence 65; relational quality 65; responsible behavior 65
turn construction unit (TCU) 34
turn-initial cues 35
turn-taking behavior 41
turn-taking protocol: adjacency pair 35; American English 37–40; contextual factors 41–43; in conversations 34–35; cross-culture practice 40–41; cross-language practice 40–41; Mandarin Chinese 36–37; overlapping 36; repair 36

uncertainty avoidance 119, 120
uniform accounting standards 131
unique cultural systems 7

United States: individualist orientation 64; individual personality 64; trustworthiness concept 64; US Civil Rights Act of 1964 88
unit of speech 34
US businesspeople: personal integrity 65, 68; trustworthiness groupings 67
US Civil Rights Act of 1964 88
US Equal Employment Opportunity Commission 88

valence dimension 23
value calm states (LAP) 31
value excitement states (HAP) 25, 31
values, cultural systems 6
verbal exchanges 41
verbal expressions 27
virtual nudges 11

Wehrfritz, M. 141
Western cultures 22, 24; employee loyalty 75
women 21
work: emotions in 22; notion 65; overload 76, 81; relationship 68

work–life balance 80, 149
workplace harassment 89, 90
World Bank on Argentina (ARD) 122
worldview orientations: ascription/achievement dimension 10; cross-cultural professional interactions 13–14; hierarchy/egalitarian dimension 9–10; high-context/low-context dimension 11–12; individualism/collectivism dimension 9; mastery/adaptive dimension 12–13; monochronic/polychronic dimension 12
written responses 25–27; excited and calm emotions 26; word stems 26

xin ("trustworthiness") 82

yi ("righteousness") 81, 82

Zhang, X. 90
zhi ("wisdom") 82
Zhu, W. 15, 41, 148
Zinoviev, A. 134

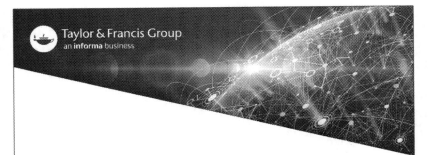

Printed in the United States
by Baker & Taylor Publisher Services